THE POWER OF PERCEPTION

WHAT DO YOU SEE
WHEN YOU LOOK AT A ROSE?

Marcus Bach

DeVorss & Company
Box 550, Marina del Rey, California 90294

Library of Congress Catalog Card Number: 66-11753
ISBN: 0-87516-523-0

Cover photographs by Lorena Bach

Printed in the United States of America

To

Hilda J. B.

"Perception Personified"

Books by Marcus Bach

THEY HAVE FOUND A FAITH

REPORT TO PROTESTANTS

FAITH AND MY FRIENDS

STRANGE ALTARS

THE DREAM GATE

THE WILL TO BELIEVE

THE CIRCLE OF FAITH

GOD AND THE SOVIETS

MAJOR RELIGIONS OF THE WORLD

ADVENTURES IN FAITH

STRANGE SECTS AND CURIOUS CULTS

HAD YOU BEEN BORN IN ANOTHER FAITH

THE UNITY WAY OF LIFE

MAKE IT AN ADVENTURE

LET LIFE BE LIKE THIS

SPIRITUAL BREAKTHROUGHS FOR OUR TIME

CONTENTS

PART TWO: THE COMMONLY UNHEARD

PART THREE: THE COMMONLY UNFELT

INTRODUCTION

Practicing the Power of Perception

An instructor in the field of archery told me about a student with a high I.Q., physically fit and with 20/20 vision, who was one of his most disappointing students in bow-and-arrow training. Usually effective teaching methods had not produced results in the case of exchange student Alfredo Gomez, whose interest in the art of archery was extra-curricular and intensive and whose major study was computer processing.

One evening, spurred by a hunch, the instructor took his pupil to the university gym. Setting the target 80 yards from the shooting area, the teacher ordered his student to prepare for a customary target shot. Alfredo positioned himself, strung the arrow into the bow, and was concentrating on the target when the instructor abruptly turned off the lights. The evening session proceeded with Alfredo addressing the target in the dark through the uncanny vision of his "mind's eye." He scored an amazing record, including two shots in the outer zone of the golden area of the bull's eye.

If you are skeptical of such sensational goings-on, try it with equipment no more complicated than a handful of darts and a dart board, as I did with startling success, enough to persuade me that the adventure offers interesting insights into the power of perception.

Beyond our five sensory aptitudes, outreaching ESP, serendipity, chance or coincidence, is the reach of an inner eye of intuition. This may or may not be the vaunted third eye or "seer" heralded in occult science and other esoteric fields, but somewhere inherent in you and me is an intrepid archer as true and fully as mysterious as the psyche which has intrigued the seekers-after-Self since the beginning of time.

Descendents of the Samurai still relate how "the arrow that is not aimed" was among the phenomena for which their ancestors were famous. These disciplined and stoic lords in the days of feudalism in Japan demonstrated incredible powers of perception. An intruder or an assailant was not discovered by sounds he made or clues he might inadvertently give as to his presence. He was "sensed" by Samurai adepts as our domesticated pet psyches out the presence of another of its kind long before it is seen, heard, scented or surmised. Animals and birds in the woodlands are aware of our presence long before we know they are there. And yet, the inner sense of our knowing is a prehensile part of our nature, sublimated only by what we call progress and time.

My Swiss mother, in recounting the legend of William Tell shooting the apple on the head of his son, never failed to add the qualifier, "The arrow was aimed by Someone greater than Tell."

We could argue that our powers of perception have been diminished because science and technology do the job for us with so much greater efficiency and stealth and speed. The human minds that brought about computers, space vehicles, lasers and the like have created a greater than Samurai world.

What is here involved in the power of perception may best be described as a reflexive flash of mind when the rational and intuitive hemispheres of the brain interact in an instant of concentration and release. While the experience known as *deja vue* —recall of past and present in synchronicity—may be roughly descriptive and similar in nature, the perceptive event we are talking about is in effect an encounter into the realm of the superconscious.

Thought is an arrow in flight. The hidden *you* is the archer.

The greatest performances are those in which the reflexive flash is carried to its highest capability, sustained, as it were, by the training and talent of concentration and release. What the rational mind has recorded in neural patterns is here intuitively released and expressed.

It is equally true to affirm that what intuition has perceived is now, in this instance, rationally proclaimed. This is why perception is defined as "the process by which a living organism becomes aware of stimuli."

I am tempted to wonder anew at how many remarkable sequences in world history fit into this targeted concept and the arrow without aim.

Consider, for example, how ancient observers, by no means scientifically skilled, had the audacity to perceive that the moon is merely the sun's reflected light and that the tides have an influence upon humankind. Long before the coming of a Galileo or Copernicus, primitive perceivers concluded that the earth is a sphere in motion and by sheer perception divined that there is an unmoved Mover of the universe. Arrows unerringly aimed by the power of perception finding their target in flight.

That there is a correlation between the flight of a self-cognitive arrow and the writing of a book became more apparent to me when THE POWER OF PERCEPTION gradually took form. As I think of it now, its development, true to the target I had in mind, was dominated by a series of "shots in the dark." My meeting with a Zen in Mandalay had been purely serendipitous. Suddenly, however, it became the very basis of all that was to follow. As you will see in Chapter 1, the monk's parting words were nothing more or less than a koan and yet they were the opening doors to practically all that was to follow. It established a storyline. It triggered an almost total recall of events and adventures that fell into place.

I remember asking myself whether, without the chance meeting in Mandalay, I would have seen the beauty of the wagon wheel and the trailing morning glory in the American midwest with which the book begins.

Shots in the dark, I concluded, are actually arrows of light, and in that consciousness a formula for the practice of perception was born.

Whether or not the archery experiment represented a valid *fait accompli*, it suggested to me that in the field of communication, the archery metaphor is highly significant. The development of a writing style is surely essential and a great deal of light has been thrown upon it in training sessions, but there is a process that takes place in the unseen that is essentially part of the craft. It is, in fact, the heart of it.

The practice of the power of perception, insofar as the writing of the book was concerned, was filled with moments when the archer within me "turned off the lights" and freed creative consciousness sufficiently to psych out untargeted events which eventually comprised a unified whole. That which was seemingly "made" into a book was mystical, and that which appeared as having been contrived was actually that which was karmically recalled.

The quiver of arrows, so to say, was obviously chapter headings such as: Intuition, Reflection, Empathy, Apprehension, and the like. The storyline fell naturally into the construct of a triad: THE COMMONLY UNSEEN, THE COMMONLY UNHEARD and THE COMMONLY UNFELT.

Looking at this triad in illustrative fashion, we discover effectively the reach of our own inner eye. There are, to begin with, a great many options. We can see things as they are, that is in the light of implacable "reality." We can see things as we might wish them to be, as we are convinced they *must* be and *can* be if we will utilize every means to make them so. We can see them as fantasies against the real or as real against the fantasy, and we may have to decide whether Plato the idealist was a realist at heart, or whether, as some say, it was the other way around. The phenomenal world and the real are up for grabs, and that is where the full challenge and charge of the commonly unseen enters the target area.

Years ago, during my research of Catholic shrines, including Lourdes, Our Lady of Guadalupe and Montserrat, the riddle of perceptive powers consistently deepened. At Fatima in Portugal a cynical tourist told me that the children who claimed to have seen the Virgin there in 1917 should have had their eyes examined. The apparition, he figured, could have been the result of a bad case of astigmatism.

In contrast to such cynicism, I recalled a visit with Professor D. T. Suzuki. I was sitting with this Zen teacher on the tatami mat in his home in Atami, Japan. I had been to Rome where a Jesuit priest told me that when the doctrine of the assumption of Mary became a dogma, he, the priest, was so happy he danced in the street.

I said to Dr. Suzuki, "What do you think of that from an intelligent, highly trained cleric? How can he be so sure that Mary ascended bodily into heaven? Who saw her?"

The Zen teacher sat for a long while in the silence as we closed our eyes in meditation at the thought. Eventually, in a soft voice, Suzuki said as if to himself, "I saw her." And I recall saying with surety, half-aloud, "I saw her too."

What do *you* see when you look at a rose and invoke the power of perception.

And what do you hear when you listen to the wind? That is Part Two of the triad: THE COMMONLY UNHEARD.

From a whispered murmur to its howling tornadic blast, there is nothing quite so mysterious, awesome or compelling as the voice or voices of the wind. Primordially, the language of the wind takes us back to something before the beginning and certainly prior to the coming of man.

To interpret the koan in such a frame of reference would be unfair, although certainly allowable; especially if your perception leads you that way.

I would rather we looked upon "the wind" as metaphysical. Let's consider it for the moment as symbolic of any perceptive stimuli awakened in our consciousness by any number of circumstances. From the whisper of a friend to a message from the cosmological Whoever or Whatever holds the harnessed winds under control or unleashes them abruptly as an arrow without aim, let's ask the question again, "What do you hear when you listen to the wind?"

During seminars on perception, I frequently ask participants to think back on an unexpected event that happened to them years ago and which, at the time, was considered especially tragic and traumatic. When I ask the question, "How many of you now look back on that confrontation or experience as a point of personal growth and new insight into life?" Invariably the consensus is that unexpected setbacks in life are not devoid of feed-forward motivations. Whether an analysis of history would bear this out is uncertain, but again, you might test the principle in your own life's experiences.

There is something in the human psyche that has the will to rationalize for good or ill depending upon the total structure of the total person.

I am thinking, as I write this in the comfort of my upstairs study in our Palos Verdes, California, home, how precisely eight months ago I was alone in the house when a freak storm struck our usually sheltered town.

I awoke on that tornadic night thinking that an earthquake was rocking this section of southern California. The house was shaking and there were crashing sounds in our always quiet neighborhood. The electric power was off, the telephones were knocked out, a driving rain with lightning and thunder were part of the Valkyric orchestration. Flashlight in hand, I ventured to step out into the patio. It was instantly clear what was happening: the wind was hoeing down the towering eucalyptus trees for which Palos Verdes is famous. The fronded giants were crashing down on homes, shattering garden walls and ripping up the yards and streets.

I look out now. I walk the streets: La Selva, Via Alameda, Via Anita, Via Colusa. There is not a house but that is lovelier now, there's not a yard but that is more kempt and trim, and by the miracle of nature and the tree trimmers' skill, the skyline of eucalyptus has never been so picturesque.

Perhaps we need an Alice in Wonderland rationale, a bit of naïvete, some good insurance, and a dogged will to believe, but something keeps telling me that the voice of the wind is very closely related to the voice of life.

The third component of the triad follows inevitably: WHAT DO YOU FEEL WHEN YOU FEEL THE COMMONLY UNFELT?

Here we are compelled to reach for something beyond words and to search in the stillness for the art of spiritual communication. The feeling suggested by this koan is psycho-sensory within ourselves no less than intrapersonally. Ann Morrow Lindbergh describes it for us in her incomparable TWO CITADELS:

> "We cannot meet, two citadels of stone,
> Imprisoned in our walls, two worlds that spin
> Each in a separate orbit, each alone,
> We are two homesteads, sheltering within
> A score of lives. A score of household selves
> Polish the floors, replenish pantry shelves,
> Ticking to duties, all the clock-told day
> Without a window-look across the way.
>
> We cannot meet, stone citadels stand fast,
> Two worlds do not embrace, homesteads are bound
> Attached to place, to time, to each day's round;
> But evenings, when the drudgery is past,
> And blinds are drawn and children safe in bed,
> And adults sit and dream and nod the head,

A child within each house can slip apart,
Run barefoot down the stairs and out to meet
His playmate. Breathless, in the dark, they greet
And fling each other wholly heart to heart."

This is the kind of stuff of which reality and dreams are made and this is the kind of thinking that refuses to differentiate between the two. I have walked home from philharmonic concerts and great performances with a sense of agonizing joy as the result of a rapport with the virtuoso or artist who lifted me to spiritual heights in the sanctuary of my hidden, sheltered life. Little did they know how deeply they touched me, how they complimented me by a secret knowing that I might understand and feel with them the commonly unfelt. The power they generated in the citadel of their life held rendezvous with the power secretly responsive in mine. Each in his own household might have had all too little in common and been all too much involved with daily chores. We might not even have gotten along or cared for each other in the workaday clock-told world, but for a little while, unattached to place or time, we met for a moment of encounter in an altered state of consciousness.

That perception generates attraction is a foregone conclusion. Send out your thoughts, and you can expect telepathic messages. Send out your feelings, and you will be rewarded in kind.

With a name like Bach I felt I had every right to become a great musician. The goal of violinist eluded me, however, on a number of counts and for a varied number of reasons. The painful nostalgia that I never made it has finally been assuaged; the love affair with my beloved fiddle is all but closed. For when the light of this ambition was abruptly turned off, arrows without aim began to manifest themselves.

At the very moment of this writing, I find that perceptive magic of thought has within the past few months drawn me to three extraordinary musicians, or drawn them to me for a purpose still to be resolved. I think they were serendipitously summoned into my orbit simply because of this new edition of the book for which this preface is written.

First among this trio of musician-composers to cross my path within the year was H. Klyne Headley of Vancouver, British Columbia. Until we met and had dinner together in the enchanted woodland of Stanley Park, his name and his renown as a concert pianist were known to me only because he had been one of the first American composers to tour a great part of the world as a guest of the State Department's Cultural Affairs activities. An American citizen, he was living in Santa Barbara, California, at the time. His performances and his ability to tap the essential universality of creative improvisation were marks of his genius.

But now all that was beside the point. The arrow without aim that had brought us together was our mutual quest for avenues or paths or side roads and even detours that led to practicing the power of perception.

Headley's credentials, beginning with a Master's Degree in music from the University of Rochester Eastman School of Music, and his quarter of a century of teaching in universities and colleges, were marked by numerous awards and citations. His compositions and his career as a concert pianist were highlighted by such masterworks as a triptych, *Peace,* written and performed for the Brensky Detsky Sbor (Children's Choir) and a Symphonic Cycle in four volumes, *Prelude to Man,* inspired by Chard Powers Smith's epic poem by the same title. Of this masterwork, Headley said, "What I have attempted, in surrounding this epic poem with music, is to supply the link between our imagination of truth and our conception of it. It seems timely that we take a macroscopic view of the universe and the great drama of man and his quest for God, rather than the microscopic view that tempts us because of external forces."

Such talent and genius might well be beyond my reach were it not for the fact that here at a table in Stanley Park and in later intimate conferences with Klyne Headley, the harmony of a common chord of creative understanding was as natural as a native language. Headley came directly to the heart of it when, to his insight into the practice of perception, he put his philosophy and approach into the following formula:

"Power, which is mind, energy and all life, furnishes the creative connection with consciousness, awareness—the very essence of being—or, in one word, perception.

"The perfect union of power and perception realizes universal creative forces inherent within all life forms.

"In the beginning is the equation: POWER plus PERCEPTION equals CREATION."

The theory has now been effectively translated by Headley into an impressive use of improvisation for healing holistically through the touch of music. He refers to his approach, and rightly so, as transfiguration through music, a therapeutic tool in meeting people's special needs.

That space and time are nonexistent to perceptive thought became self-evident when Australian composer, Walter Robins, sent me several cassettes of his original compositions with a message saying that THE POWER OF PERCEPTION had directly influenced him in his approach to tapping the source of superconsciousness as an aid to his professional career. He wanted to familiarize me with some of his compositions and philosophy. The first consisted of a monumental presentation, *North Queensland Overture*. The second was in the form of an interview in which Mr. Robins shared his philosophy and his technique for creative musical expression.

"There is in man," Robins confided to his interviewer, "only one true source of original composition. This source is to be found in man's superconsciousness and not in his conscious workaday mind. The great composers of history instinctively drew on this creativity from deep within without consciously acknowledging the fact or, in some documented cases, actually were aware of and drew upon this source. I myself have through meditation tapped my superconsciousness with gratifying results."

He illustrated his point by citing evidence from three master musicians of the past. "Joseph Hayden," Robins explained, "worked in terms of a virtual 'ritual.' He always dressed up in his best clothes before commencing to work. And he said, 'I am now going to commune with God and I must be perfectly dressed,' When asked how he was able to create such marvelous music, Hayden replied, 'When I decide to compose, I pray and begin by thanking God that it has been accomplished. Then I do it. If it doesn't come the first time, I try again. Then it comes.' Hayden had to perceive a higher level than himself before he could compose successfully."

"Mozart, when he was asked about the process of composition, said, 'The process with me is like a beautiful, vivid dream.' He went on to describe how the ideas clothed in the proper musical setting streamed down upon him. 'Of course,' he warned, 'the composer must also have mastered the technique of his art, the basics.' What Mozart was trying to tell us is that the difference between the mere technician and the genius is found in the perception of the vivid dream.

" 'When I feel well,' Mozart continued, 'and am in good humor, or when I am taking a drive or walking, thoughts crowd into my mind as easily as you could wish. How or whence they come I do not know. I have nothing to do with it. Once I have a theme another melody comes, linking itself with the first one in accordance with the needs of the composition as a whole. Now my soul is on fire with inspiration. The work grows, expanding more and more clearly until I have the composition as I perceive it. My imagination lets me hear it in its entirety."

Referring to Beethoven, Robins quoted from one of the composer's letters, that he was unsure of the source of his creativity, yet he went on to refer to the mind of nature and that his inspirational ideas came unbidden. Beethoven's letter reported, "I carry my ideas about with me for a long time and often a very long time before I write them down. In doing so, my memory is so trustworthy that I am sure I will never forget a theme, even after a period of years, once I have committed it to memory. I hear and see the work in my mind, as though in proportion, as already accomplished. All that remains now is the labor of writing it out. This proceeds quickly depending on the time I have available since I often have several pieces at which I work at once. You ask where I get my ideas. They come indirectly, directly. I could grasp them with my hands. The mind of nature, in the woods on walks, in the silence of the night, in the early mornings inspired by moods that translate themselves as the words of a poet. The sounds surge, roar and at last they stand before me as notes."

Robins believes that true inspiration comes from tapping the superconscious and the process for him is to enter this stage through meditation. His music bears tremendous testimony to the practical workability of his technique.

If the Headley connection in Vancouver and the Robins' contact in Queensland were unsolicited, it must follow that a communication from a highly skilled technician in musicology, William B. Conner, of Allentown, Pennsylvania, was equally unexpected and must have been borne on the same psychically perceptive wings. Conner's letter informed me that he had been inspired by an article I had written in *Fate Magazine* long ago, bearing upon a certain aspect of creativity. Accompanying his letter were two incredible published works under his authorship, MUSIC'S METASONICS and MATH'S METASONICS. To me both documents were the work of a mind far beyond mine. Evidently this scholar out of the Keystone State was a modern Pythagoras with a liberal touch of Aristotelian metaphysics. My correspondence and research found William B. Conner listed in the Directory of American Scholars and in Men of Achievement as a linguist of academic note and a scientist who had been responsible for the Tonalingua-Concordophone system; the latter being a process which enhances coloristic poetry through addition of color, light and chordal sound combinations.

There was now no doubt in my mind about perception's power to bring together three contemporary creative composers in the field of music and permitting me to recognize myself as the catalyst for perception's plans, no matter whatever they might be.

Press coverage of Conner's works focused on the awareness that there is a creative consciousness in which scientific facts are one and the same, and in which chemical elements, nature, and the entire universe are comprehended in musical tones and mathematical harmonics.

Conner links the miracle of meditation with the mystery of creative thought when he proposes that object-events emerge from frequencies, and these are beyond space-time. It is theorized that at "Ground Zero" (the implicate order) all possible orderings into the explicate order (the world of Form) are present. Put into the oceanic metaphor, God's centering Stillness lies in the deeps. Only the ocean's surface activates Motion and Space (for Motion to exist in terms of Here-to-There) and Time (for Motion to exist in terms of This Moment-Later Moment). All thought springs from the electromagnetic surface of this ocean, not from the deeps. However, all Cause lies in the infinite potential frequencies of the Divine Light spectrum. All Cause inheres in the infinite potential frequencies of the Ocean's depths.

You will agree with me, I am sure, that the trio of these contemporary music composers matches the triad proclaimed in THE POWER OF PERCEPTION, namely seeing the Commonly Unseen, hearing the Commonly Unheard and feeling the Commonly Unfelt. They reveal themselves as unified in an integrated whole.

From arrows without aim to music from some subliminal source, the full discovery of our link to the unknown Source of Allness lies all around us in every field of human research and endeavor. The pages that follow are in essence targets for one's own inner challenges, whatever our time or talent on planet Earth may be. The mystic, William Blake, said it so well, that I will let it stand, "If the doors of perception were cleansed everything would appear to man as it is, infinite."

—Marcus Bach, Ph.D.
Palos Verdes Estates, California.
(1983)

PART ONE

THE COMMONLY UNSEEN

I * INSIGHT

One spring morning I parked my car on a country road and got out to look at an old familiar scene: a broken wagon wheel that someone long ago had propped up to close a gap in a stretch of weathered rail fence. Often when I had driven by in winter I had noticed the wheel draped with snow and ice, and in summer a quick glance assured me that nature used it as a trellis for whatever had a wish to grow there.

This time I stopped. So did other travelers. The farmer who owned the place stood there smiling, puzzled and surprised as he glanced from a newspaper in his hand to the wheel and the fence. I had seen the paper, too, with its report that an itinerant photographer had won a thousand-dollar prize with a photo of the fractured wheel entwined by a morning glory vine and showing in the distance a herd of cattle silhouetted against the hills and sky.

He had titled his picture "Homestead" and his photographic skill caused us to visualize a cavalcade of wagons rolling across these midwestern fields, conjured up the march of the pioneer, suggested the passing of time and the bounty of the land in which one segment of America worked and served and found the things which they considered good and beautiful and true.

It was all there in the wheel and the fence and I left the place thoughtfully and a bit frustrated, for I carry a camera, too, and have never won anything more than an honorable mention which, just now, seemed quite dishonorable, considering how often I had passed this scene without so much as clicking the shutter. I could also have used the thousand dollars but consoled myself with the thought that if the laborer is worthy of his hire, then he who sees the commonly unseen is surely justified in his reward.

Finding life's thinly veiled wonders

It was not only photography that was involved here, it was life, for certainly the art of living includes the ability to see the unobvious, and part of life's adventure is to respond creatively to that which is ordinarily unobserved. Other techniques there may be, as there are in all fields of art, but the basic one—the inner sight—this, I now realized, can add a new dimension to our day-by-day experiences.

I walked back to my car reflecting on the fact that I needed to view my world more closely, respond to it more deeply, and interpret things more creatively in order to find the wonders so thinly veiled from sight.

I drove away wondering how many other scenes I had passed by, all the way from experiences I had failed to analyze to the seemingly inconsequential happenings in which I was frequently involved. How many "awards" had I missed by failing to see the unseen? How many events and circumstances had I taken for granted when, with a bit of imagination and insight, I could have widened the circumference of my world? I had been so busy traveling the road that I often overlooked some obvious opportunities and forfeited the inspirations which my inner vision could easily have relayed to me.

I should have known this all along, for once in Mandalay a respected Buddhist teacher, a monk who became my friend, challenged me by saying, "What do you see when you look at a rose?" To which he added, "What do you hear when you listen to the wind, and what do you feel when you feel the commonly unfelt?"

It was his way of affirming that every event has an undiscovered meaning, every experience is a pressure point directed toward some new and greater unfoldment, and every situation has a significancein-depth leading into a fuller awareness of potentials hidden deep within oneself.

Yes, I should have known this, especially since my field of research revolved around the beliefs and philosophies that people live by in almost every part of the world. For more than twenty exciting years I had been investigating the intriguing paths by which people of various cultures arrived at their deepest convictions.

The scale of my research ran literally from A to Z, from the Animist in primitive parts of Asia to the Zoroastrian in India. One insisted that he could see a spiritual force in every stick and stone in nature and in himself; the other was convinced that good and evil were actual forces, struggling to gain control of the soul of man. Why did they believe these things? An inner sight, an inner vision, they said, had given them a special revelation, and this was the justification for every deep-seated belief in every culture. Insight! *Someone had seen the commonly unseen.* This was the basis of faith.

Evidently faith was the willingness to perceive a thought and a will infinitely larger than one's own. Faith was the ability to see what others had failed to see, or to discover what others had vainly hoped to see. And this was why in recent years I had become more introspective. Instead of investigating others, I was asking myself what conclusions I had come to and where I stood as far as my own place in this matter of insight was concerned.

As I drove from the country road to a sparkling new highway which followed an old route over which I had often gone, I could not help paraphrasing the Buddhist's question about the rose. "What do you see when you look at a super-highway?" I asked myself. "What do you see in the traffic? In the frantic rush of a restless people or in the affluence and industry of a nation on the move?" What did I see in the cars and trucks in the network of freeways, turnpikes, and parkways of America and in the changing scenes through which my morning's ride was taking me?

The personal point of view

It dawned on me how vital and personal the choice of a point of view can be. By a twist of the mind I could create almost any type of world as I traveled on. True, there were conditions round about me that were real enough and over which I apparently had no control, but by the magic of applied insight I could find new meaning and responses in my surroundings as surely as the cunning photographer had found a new angle in a broken wheel and an old rail fence.

"What do you see when you look at a rose?" The words linked East and West in a moment of reflection. As the photographer had seen the wheel and related it to America, so my friend in Mandalay saw life and related it to the unseen. Long before photography was born, philosophers carried cameras-of-the-mind and used their skill to make us pause and re-examine the roads we travel, urging us to take a second look at old familiar scenes along the way.

Talk about the power of suggestion! As I drove along I had the feeling that my car was suddenly filled with passengers whose names had not occurred to me since college days; shopworn names, bringing to life such old-timers as Socrates, Plato, Aristotle, joining my Buddhist friend and me for a ride along a newly finished thoroughfare.

Perhaps my educational process had been faulty or there was something wrong with me, but up until now I had never taken these men too seriously. I had put them into a special category as though they were people apart. They weren't. They were itinerant photographers of the soul, individuals like ourselves, but with sharpened observation, trying to find their way through the complicated world of their time. They were sages and seers, just as we are, seeking to explain the past or get a fresh glimpse of the future by taking another look at a wheel or a rose.

As they rode with me in the whir of traffic, U.S.A., somehow they were not so shopworn any more.

I used to have the impression that philosophers had all the answers. They didn't. They had their questions just as we have, and they went through life asking them over and over, running them through their minds as thoughtfully as a child lets sand run through his hands. They looked for solutions with no less wonder and frustration than we do and usually they came to no final conclusion other than a searching glance from earth to sky. But they knew the secret of trying to see the commonly unseen. They developed insight. This was their greatness and life was their quest.

So I rode along in a world strangely transformed on an old route remarkably new.

A pollster once reported that in America two thirds of our most creative thinking takes place behind the wheel of a car. Just now I agreed and urged my unseen philosopher friends to make themselves as comfortable as they could while they shared with me thoughts and truths which once had seemed as dry as academic dust. Now when they insisted that there is a good deal more to our world and to our being in the world than meets the eye, I had the will to listen. Hadn't I just seen a wheel and a fence?

Behind the things we call the real, they saw a greater reality and beyond the perishable things of life they caught a vision of something that never dies. Urging men to get the feeling of worlds beyond this world and to gear their thinking to this awareness, they suggested that each new day is a time for search and discovery.

"My mother," said Socrates, "was a midwife, and I am following her profession. I am a mental midwife, helping others to give birth to their ideas."

"I see," said Plato, "a more extraordinary being within myself than the one I permit myself to be. Perhaps I am a plaything in the hands of God, a toy in which he has delight."

He did not mean a plaything or a toy in the sense that God had him on a string or that a divine power wound him up and eventually let him run down and die. He meant that he, like every other person, was a particular expression of God for a certain period in time and space and that nothing could be more wonderful than to play one's highest part. It was not a final conclusion by any means. It was a speculation, a road stop along the highway of the quest.

"This non-material side of life," said Aristotle, "is man's true, thinking self, with capabilities far beyond his knowing. The physical world and man's physical nature are unspeakably wonderful, but the soul is the real and the truly real is the soul."

I had never actually known these men. They had been presented to me in academic caps and gowns, locked in ivory towers, but they were never comfortable there, and I was never comfortable with them. Now as they seemed to ride with me along a white-marked lane in the traffic-crowded highway of my American way of life, I found them good companions with a talent for spotting the broken wheels and the fences and a remarkable genius for taking me back to scenes and circumstances whose deepest meaning I had missed along the way.

Trying to understand greatness

Just now, I felt the same way about Jesus, and I imagined that He, too, rode with me, not in a religious or sectarian sense, but simply as One whose life and teachings I could not escape; One, who in spite of all my study and training in theological schools, had never seemed quite real, had never come to life, real life of the kind that I felt called upon to live. I used to sing about Him and pray about Him and talk about Him a good deal, but He remained something of a myth. The more I tried to fit Him into my environment, the more His myth-like quality increased. Who was He and how was I to deal with Him in a world far different from the unhurried pastoral world of Nazareth?

Once in a course in religion a professor asked me to read a portion of the Sermon on the Mount. He wanted it projected with feeling so that its poetic quality would "dramatically shine through."

I remembered how reverently I opened the Good Book to the incomparably beautiful text in the King James version: "And seeing the multitude He went up into a mountain. . . ." I knew the words from memory. I had been brought up on them. I could recite the passages verbatim from the first Beatitude to the closing line. So I read—with feeling—words which had been gospel for me since the days of my boyhood. Only this time I had an impulse to stop and, turning to the professor, I asked, "How can we do it?"

"Do what?" he wanted to know.

"Love our enemies. . . . walk the second mile. . . . judge not. . . . take no thought of the morrow?"

"Read," he said. "That is all I asked you to do."

Read. Project. Communicate. But what about insight?

Didn't the professor know that times had changed in ways which the Galilean with all His divinity and wisdom had not foreseen? Couldn't he see that we were being asked to put this unworkable first-century idealism into our twentieth-century world and that it could not be done? Or could it?

It was not the language or the analogies that Jesus used that made the problem and the dilemma so acute. Most of us knew what He meant when He talked about entering a narrow gate or walking the way called "straight." When He referred to the lilies of the field, we remembered that we had seen lilies of some sort, if only in a florist's window. We had a rough idea what it was like to have a mote in one's eye and what was meant by hiding a light under a bushel. We even had a hunch about His reference to the salt of the earth. Yes, we got along fairly well with the language. The crux of the problem had to do with actions and attitudes in a world that was as different from the world of Galilee as truck traffic on an American highway is different from burros on a cobbled road.

Whether we liked it or not, we were now living in an era where the concepts presented by the Man on the Mount were no longer as important or as disturbing or as authoritarian as they had been in the days of the world He knew. Yet we continued to make believe that what He said was valid for our time and, in so doing, a sense of dishonesty and unreality had become part and parcel of our faith. There was a growing gap between what we professed and what we practiced, and we were hiding behind a symbolism of language out of which the meaning had gone.

If we truly tried to live the words, what then? What would actually happen if we turned the other cheek or walked the second mile or loved our enemies? A noted scholar, Alfred North Whitehead, answered the question flatly by saying, "As society is now constituted, a literal adherence to the moral precepts in the Gospels would mean sudden death!"

"Read," said the professor. "That is all I asked you to do."

Then came a day. A day like the day of the wheel or the rose, when the fullness of time comes quietly into a questing heart.

How it comes or why it comes can hardly be explained. It simply happens or perhaps we make it happen by seeing the unseen or by opening an inner door or by merely pausing to look once more at an old familiar scene with a maturing glance. Or is it the reward of insight? Yes, that by all means, an answer to the invitation to come into a quiet place or on to a highway swarming with people on the move, people on the job, people traveling, endlessly traveling, doing their heavy thinking behind the wheels of their cars.

At any rate, there came a day when something told me He was really quite approachable and that I could share my thoughts with Him without seeming either presumptuous or naïve.

It was more than an "act of grace," as the theologians would say. In a way it was a minor miracle, this matter of bringing the Nazarene out of the clouds of doctrinal captivity and discovering that one could sit with Him even as those whom He loved sat with Him in Bethphage and Bethany, and that one could ride with Him at seventy miles an hour along a busy traffic-crowded lane in the heart of the U.S.A.

The quest impelled by an ideal

What did He say? How did He justify the ground rules of the game He played; suggestions about being different, about demonstrating a new sense of values, of being in the world and not of the world? The answer was simple enough when one heard Him present it without any dogmatic overtones or any coaching from those who insisted on putting some profound, inscrutable meaning into His simple words. "It is a quest," He made clear, and He thought it a good idea to challenge men to express their indwelling spirit no matter where or when they lived and to let that spirit travel as far as a man's will and consciousness and faith allowed it to go.

Was it easy, this quest for a higher, more adventurous life? No, nothing worth-while is ever easy. Was it realizable? Partially. Nothing idealistic is ever fully realized. Was it possible to live as He advised? Only to the degree that one was willing and able to see the commonly unseen. Could we escape the impulse of trying to reach the ideal? No. Haunted by His challenge, tantalized by a driving force of faith, spurred by the knowledge that we have a capacity for goodness far beyond our reach, we would be untrue to ourselves if we settled for less than our best. Insight! Clearly it was a matter of insight.

Suddenly the myth had meaning, as all myths have, and slowly the Figure that had been hazy and ephemeral came to life, even as did the philosophers when I took them at their word.

I came back full circle to Whitehead who had said that anyone living according to the Gospel's precepts was courting "sudden death." Like all men of serious thought and honesty, he had a qualification for his views. "The progress of humanity," he said, "can be defined as the process of transforming society so as to make the Christian ideals practicable for its members."

That was it. It *was* a quest and we *were* being impelled by an ideal. An adventurous world *did* exist for those who were willing to see the commonly unseen.

For a moment I felt a nearness to every other driver who sat behind his wheel on this highway of life. Whatever his thoughts, I shared them. Whatever his experience, it was mine. Whatever his level of insight, I felt I could understand. Here we were, people of every type in vehicles of every kind, endlessly moving, part of the swinging lanes of hypnotic sights and sounds while the spring sunlight caught us in our speeding metal shafts. A symphonic rhythm ran through it all, the rhythm of a country caught in progress and in thought.

The old philosophers, to whom I owed a debt, made way for the later ones who owed a debt to them. Their once unpronounceable names returned: Malebranche, Schleiermacher, Wittgenstein,

Kirkegaard . . . Hegel, Spinoza, Kant, Aquinas, Berkeley . . . to say nothing of the analysts like Freud, Jung, Adler, and Fromm. They made quite a carful and I heard them philosophizing and debating as they had throughout my seemingly endless academic years.

"I must reconsider everything that I have ever learned and believed," murmured René Descartes. "All that I have accepted as true and certain was learned through the senses. Now I realize that these senses are not enough. They have been deceptive and it is wiser not to trust entirely something by which I have once been deceived."

"When I am in trouble," Kant spoke up, "should I make a promise though I have no intention of keeping it? And what happens when my action becomes a universal code of behavior?"

"The total expression of human experience," exclaimed William James, "is beyond any narrow or ethical bounds. The real world is of a different temperament and more intricately built than physical science allows. It is a world unseen!"

"The unseen in man is his psyche," said Jung. "This is the shadow with which he must make his peace."

Suddenly I saw a harmony in the seemingly disharmonious schools of thought and sensed a point that my early teachers had surely missed: all philosophers, no matter how or where they disagreed, believed that life is a quest, a road to be traveled, and each sought to reveal as best he could his vision of the commonly unseen.

Insight! Everyone had it, but not everyone used it. Many people carried cameras but only occasionally did one snap the shutter on the broken wheel and the fence. An endless stream of individuals poured in and out of colleges, clinics, churches, and retreats, and I along with them, but only rarely did one awaken to the unseen within himself and the yet-to-be-discovered-world in which we lived!

The substance of the unseen

What do you see when you look at a rose? And who rides with you when you ride alone?

Philosophers are easy to come by. You can find them on every college campus and in every library and bookshop, even in racks bulging with popular magazines. As for the Galilean, He has been talked about and quoted more than any man. But somehow when we ride alone, our thoughts continually turn to those who like ourselves are subject to the same crossflow of life that touches us. In them too and in their experiences we find insight and direction for ourselves.

My thoughts brought an authoress friend of mine, Georgiana Tree West, into the car. College classrooms may not have heard of her, and her books may never be put on required reading lists, but she had a way of seeing the commonly unseen and once during her quest she said, "Walking down Fifth Avenue I tried to see in my imagination what it must have been like 500 years ago. A wooded island. A deer might have been grazing where the Empire State Building now stands. An Indian squaw might have been gathering firewood in a little clearing that is now Rockefeller Center. What would she have thought if by some miracle she had found herself suddenly walking with me down Fifth Avenue today? Where were all of today's amazing things back in the sixteenth century? They existed potentially in the realm of the Unseen. The substance of the Unseen, which is the spiritual substance of the universe, has always been ready to pour itself into any idea that man might conceive and so project itself into form. The potentiality of everything our twentieth century boasts and everything that future civilizations can produce has always existed in the mind of God."

That was quite an insight and suggested the ability to look at life as unfolding and unlimited as well as the art of seeing ourselves as channels for the expression of a creative mind.

An elderly man, James Walker, came to ride with me in my reverie when I remembered how he had said, "I love people, animals, birds, plants, and flowers, and live to express the joy of the abundant life. I find delight in visiting lonely men and women, if they want me, and to bring some sunshine into their lives. I love art and the classics. I have painted two water colors and am altogether a most happy man of nearly three quarters of a century of years.

These things I do even though for thirty years I have been blind, only able to tell day from night. However, by turning from all evidences of the material senses to the Inner Light, I truly see. We are what we think and all that is created perfect and harmonious in mind becomes perfect and harmonious in the objective world."

And what was I to do with my little worries and concerns in the light of such a point of view?

My fantasy also picked up Michael Dunn and, heaven knows, he took up little room. Three feet, ten inches tall, weighing less than eighty pounds, he sprang to mind and rode with me. Though my meeting with him in New York had been brief and informal, I had seen him in *The Ballad of the Sad Cafe* and, like every member of every audience, I laughed and wept and wondered at the spell he wove. He made us realize that a dwarf can be a giant and live greatly in a world scaled to the size of larger men. It was his unseen life that put him in perspective. His I.Q. was that of a genius. A classical scholar no less than an astonishing actor, he stood in the world of his inner life as straight and tall as any man.

Light in darkness

Do people of this kind, I wondered, live among us to teach us how to rise above our problems and complaints? Is it possible that what analysts seek to do for us and often fail at doing, we can do for ourselves merely by seeing our unseen self through grateful eyes?

A loyal Japanese companion made his presence felt. Many times he had been my interpreter and guide, and he had a habit of submerging himself in whatever caught his attention. A piece of calligraphy was to Colbert Kurokawa not merely a form of writing to be admired, but a work in which an artist expressed his deepest self, yet a simple neon sign intrigued him, too. Life intrigued him. He was determined to follow the historic lines of the unseen until he found their creative source, a practice that accounted for his phenomenal knowledge and his mental skill.

From an Albert Schweitzer who, during my visit with him in Africa, impressed upon me the conviction that all life is a reflection of the divine, to a ranger on a Canadian summit watchtower who saw in the lightning's flash the signature of God, the allurement and transforming power of seeing the unseen became ever more graphic. From Animist to Zoroastrian, from philosopher to itinerant photographer, insight was their greatness and life was the quest.

To see the unseen! To see light when apparently there is only darkness, hope when there is seemingly nothing but despair, faith when it is crowded out by fear, the hint of joy when it appears there can never be anything but sorrow, victory in the shattering hour of defeat, and love when all seems engulfed by hate! Give me that vision, for that which I see is that which unalterably comes to pass!

But now the melee of traffic increased. Green lacquered signs of the super-highway advised me that the city I was headed for was close at hand and that I had a selection of a number of ramps to reach my destination. Thanks to the skill of engineers and those who build the roads, I would be exactly on time.

A jet from a near-by airport roared upward through a tangle of shimmering clouds. A helicopter churned lazily overhead. Trucks and cars in a fairyland of motion criss-crossed in the lanes and overpasses, while the white smoke of industry wove a spell around the skyline of the sprawling city. This was America where East and West, dreams and realities blended into a way of life.

A country road or a highway, a farmyard or a city street, prophets or just plain people, the unseen was the real.

The monk in Mandalay who had asked me to consider the rose had also given me an intriguing line: "GOD SAID, 'I HAVE MADE YOU NEITHER MORTAL NOR IMMORTAL, NEITHER EARTHLY NOR HEAVENLY, SO THAT YOU YOURSELF, AS THE MOLDER AND SHAPER OF YOUR DESTINY, MAY FASHION YOURSELF INTO WHATEVER FORM YOU BELIEVE YOURSELF TO BE.'"

Nowhere had this statement ever seemed so true or challenging as it did just then in the heart of the U.S.A.

II * REFLECTION

One day I sat in a darkened laboratory where a scientist friend had invited me to share in the demonstration of a newly constructed electronic microscope. Turning off the last remaining light in the high-ceilinged room, he adjusted the delicate controls and projected an image which completely covered a 6′×6′ beaded screen.

I was confronted by a maze of colored designs that might have been anything from a moon shot to an abstract painting. Or it could have been an aerial photograph of Yellowstone Park with its geysers and sizzling paint pots.

My guesses ran out and I asked for an explanation. My friend switched off the microscope and turned on the lights.

"See for yourself," he said, taking the glass slide out of the instrument and handing it to me.

I held the thin, narrow panel up to the light, turned it this way and that, and saw nothing.

"Mystery," I said.

The scientist agreed with an understanding nod. Then he said, "You are looking at an evidence of life."

"Which means?"

"You are seeing the ordinarily unseen. On this plate is an enzyme, invisible to the naked eye. Let's put it back and take another look into its soul."

The sliver of apparently clear glass was returned to the instrument. Once more under the probing power of magnification, the enzyme became a veritable universe with a solar system all its own. Once more the concealed world of a living organism lay bare before our gaze. We *were* looking into its soul, the soul of a substance so small you could put 10,000 on the point of a pin. Yet one alone, isolated, proved to be a creation of such compelling magnitude that it filled the room.

"Someday," said my friend half to himself, "we will be able to look into the source of life."

Later he put a virus on a glass slide. Again nothing was visible until the microscope exposed it boldly on the waiting screen. Now it could be seen and studied. Now its colors could be examined, its form analyzed, its action charted so clearly that its habits could be understood.

Silently I sat and watched. I said, "If an enzyme or a virus which cannot ordinarily be seen is the kind of giant organism we have just observed, what about you and me?"

"A good question," he replied. "But isn't that in your department?"

Looking into the souls of things

His interest was scientific; mine, metaphysical. As I sat in the spell of the darkened room, it occurred to me that what this researcher had done with the "unseen," God was continually doing with the life of man, putting our undiscovered self into the microscope of some divine awareness and projecting it on the white screen of honest investigation; God stripping us down until we saw our true essence no matter how little, if anything, we had previously seen with the "naked eye."

Reflection has many meanings. It has to do with the wonderful world around us no less than with the world within. In each case we are asked to look once more into the soul of things, including the soul of self. When we do, when we catch hold of a realization that there is always something hidden, always something yet to be discovered, always goals beyond our goals, and meanings beyond the obvious—then, for a little while, life becomes transformed.

"O world invisible, we
view thee,
O world intangible, we
touch thee,
O world unknowable, we
know thee,
Inapprehensible, we
clutch thee!"

So said Francis Thompson, in *In No Strange Land*, during a moment of inspiration, and just now the words did not seem too out of place as I thought of them in terms of "my department."

The fantastic microscope convinced me that we do not really see ourselves until we see the unlimited consciousness within ourselves. We do not realize our potentialities until we see that. We do not really know ourselves until we know that. A soul, whatever it is, dwells in us as life and we have failed to recognize it. The real "you," the innermost "I" is not really a human being, it is a projection of a deeper reality of which the "I" is but one of the subjective states of expression.

I remembered how one day, while I was writing in my cabin in British Columbia, a spider slid down from the ceiling on its gossamer thread. It was microscopically small, no larger than the point of my well-sharpened pencil, comparable, in fact, to the size of a dot which the pencil would ordinarily make. Lowering itself to the yellow sheets on which I was writing, this living speck paused as if wondering what these lines and configurations meant, or perhaps it was communicating telepathically through a secret wave frequency with some greater consciousness up there from where it had come. I touched it with my pencil. It scurried away. I approached it again, but before I could make contact, some inner response had already forewarned it that danger was near. It sped to safety, concealing itself beneath the hexagonal edge of a pencil lying on the desk.

I did not need to be an arachnidologist, as spider experts are grandiosely called, to know that in this tiny pinpoint of life that lowered itself out of space, in this minute dot that glided down on a wisp of thread created out of its own substance, in this whatever it is that we call a spider, are found intelligence, emotion, self-preservation, thought, hunger, sex, creativity; in short, life with meaning, purpose, and design. In an insect no larger than a grain of sand, the mechanism of existence was intricately housed! And here was I, six-feet-two, a sound 180 pounds, afraid at times to meet my world. My department indeed!

What was this invisible world round about me that I saw but partially and comprehended only by way of speculation? A salamander can grow a tail if one is lost, bees can determine the sex of their next hatching, the flour beetle has a built-in regulator for determining the size of its brood to meet its population needs. It was well and good to say glibly that bats are radar equipped or that the swallows return regularly to Capistrano on St. Joseph's Day, March 19, but here was I, a human being possessed of a power to destroy or control the lives of creatures whose mysteries I had never grasped. Here was I, presuming to govern and control them and often failing to control myself; I could outwit, outguess, and outlive most of them and yet I seemed incapable of tapping the rich resources within myself. No wonder I was urged to reflection!

The wonders of the commonplace

I recalled a friend who was a friend of George Washington Carver, and who spoke of this noted American botanist so affectionately that I felt I knew him, too. Imprinted on my mind was the image of Carver seated on a backless wooden bench at the edge of a sleepy plantation, holding a peanut in his hand. He was awake and alert. Everything about him was concentrated on that goober as he studied it with wondering eyes. The world with all its mysteries and revelations was captured and compressed in that simple object lying in his wrinkled palm.

"What are you studying, Mr. Carver?"

"God's Bible."

"Why, no. It's only a peanut."

"When I understand the nature of the peanut, I will understand the nature of God."

Finding its "nature," Carver made the lowly goober king over a dozen thriving industries. Industrial diamonds, linoleum, wood stains, plastics, fibers, cosmetics, medicines, candies, margarine, and other foods were conjured from the tiny peanut and its shell. Against the backdrop of the plantation I saw as on a beaded screen teeming factories and industrial plants which Carver had created through reflection and insight. Once more I saw him on the backless bench seeing the commonly unseen.

A distant cousin of the goober, the Asian soybean, was also waiting for someone to discover its inner nature. Not long ago it was considered fit for nothing more than feed for cattle and hogs. But men began to reflect on it and researchers set to work, and one day I met Howard Roach, chairman of the board of the Soybean Council of America. He invited me during one of my trips abroad to drop in at the Council's offices in Rome, London, Lisbon, Madrid, Tel Aviv, in fact, in any sizable city along the itinerary of my tour.

In these offices I saw dramatic displays of what had happened to the once despised soybean. I was shown how it had created worldwide industries and established global fellowships in research and development. I learned that back in the depths of the depression, in the thirties, Henry Ford once gave a luncheon in which everything on the menu from soup to dessert came from the humble soybean.

Ford foresaw that this legume, rotting in many a foreign field, bore within itself a great deal more than the sixteen delicacies served at his luncheon. He had invited his guests to brief them on the fact that the plastics used in Ford cars, from gearshifts to steering wheels, came from the same source as did the food which they had enjoyed. In Rome I found displays of these gears and wheels together with more than 200 other items, all the way from antibiotics to an anti-knock gasoline that had lain latent in the soybean until some creative genius tapped the power of the commonly unseen. What, I wondered, lay beneath *my* feet, and what would I discover if I reflected on the impounded wonders of the commonplace?

Great philosophies change the world, to be sure, but great inventions and discoveries change it, too, and who is to say which is the greater as far as the life of man is concerned? Was not our culture determined fully as much by our standard of living as by our standard of thought? And were not the two inseparable?

God and technology

As God once revealed Himself philosophically and theologically to the ancient world, so He reveals Himself mechanistically and technologically today. Our scientists and technicians are as influential in our life as were the prophets and priests of an older era, and each is linked to the other by the nature of their reflection on things unseen.

Think of an Isaiah or a Jeremiah confronted by the sound and sight of radio and TV! In their day they dreamed of the possibility of the voice of God being transmitted around the world of their time.

Think of the Psalmist catching a glimpse of Early Bird and relating it to the majesty of the Almighty in the brilliance of the Milky Way! What would the Psalmist's prayers and praises have been like had he but known how man would one day fill the skies!

Ezekiel saw the wheels and believed that he had insight to a world beyond his world. To him this was divine revelation. What would he say about the revelations given to our astral physicists as they follow the courses charted by our modern sciences?

Jesus spoke of the power of faith and used a mustard seed to prove His point. Holding it in His hand, He told His followers that if they had this kind of trust in the unseen they could remove mountains. Today our nuclear experts, unlocking the energy of the atom, have demonstrated mechanistically that the power of any seed, properly harnessed, can remove any number of mountains through the spectacular unleashing of its imprisoned force. What prophets of old saw metaphysically according to the laws of faith, modern researchers now demonstrate according to the laws of science. The secret in each is the same: tap and release the power of the commonly unseen!

My department indeed!

An enzyme projected on the screen persuaded me beyond a doubt that there are undiscovered areas and potentials in every life. To live in the knowledge of this gives life its zest. To see this with the "inner eye," is the supreme adventure. To have the courage to look upon oneself with this kind of vision is the challenge that at one time or other comes to each of us.

"A man grows religious by means of reflection," said Albert Schweitzer, and he did not mean religious in the sense of an institutionalized expression. He meant a oneness with all life and an awareness with the unseen. By "reflection" he meant the transmission of light and truth, as if through his own commitment in Lambarene he hoped to urge others to let their greatest and their best be projected on life's screen.

He seemed to have found himself so easily and discovered his place in the scheme of things with such simple submission that he made it look easy.

Do we strive too hard?

Is it possible, I wondered, that we strive too hard? Do we perhaps achieve more by quiet reflection than by frantic action? Can we by recognizing a rhythm and a oneness with the universe unlock our own secret doors to a new and richer life? Successful people in every field from science to sports always make greatness look easy. They are always in rhythm when they are at their best. They are partners with the unseen and their greatest aptitude is an easy acceptance of their endowments, as if what they possessed was rightfully theirs by their very willingness to receive and utilize it.

A Canadian physician, Dr. R. M. Bucke, once said that when we are in tune with a "consciousness of the cosmos" we become members of a new species. "It is then," he affirmed, "that we feel an added state of moral exaltation, an indescribable feeling of elation and joyousness, a quickening of the moral sense, which is fully as striking and more important than any enhanced intellectual power. With these faculties come what may be called a sense of immortality, a consciousness of eternal life, not a conviction that we shall have this, but the consciousness that we have it already."

He called it "Cosmic Consciousness" and wrote about it in a book under that title, citing the fact that illumination or inner awareness is the hallmark of the truly great and that the truly great are those who have the ability to see and know the commonly unseen.

Seated in the laboratory, seeing the invisible enzyme as though it were a universe, convinced me that a person can experience a consciousness of the cosmos by contemplating on the inner man or outer space, by gazing through the eye of a microscope or a telescope; either way, reflection brings us graphically into direct relationship with worlds unseen.

This was made clear to me one day when I was asked to speak at an educational meeting following a thrilling presentation by a team of science researchers. They were "Spacemobile" lecturers appearing on college and university campuses and had brought with them mock-ups and models of launch vehicles and numerous mechanical and electronic devices which held their audiences enthralled.

Presenting the basic principles of orbits and propulsion, the researchers traced the history of rocketry from the Chinese in the thirteenth century straight through to America's noted Dr. Robert Goddard and his experiments with liquid fuel. They told the story of our spacecraft, Tiros, Syncom, Ranger, Echo, Gemini, Apollo, and many more.

At one point in the program one of the men showed the audience a spacecraft computer and enumerated its intricate functions and capabilities. Explaining that it had been made eight years ago, that it weighed some sixteen pounds, measured twelve by twenty inches and was four inches thick, he impressed us with the achievement in electronic research only to show us another computer which did the same job, but which was less than half the size and weight of the former. This one, he explained, had been designed and made *four* years ago.

Then he displayed a still smaller version, a computer so compact that he dramatically drew it out of his inside pocket. It was the size of an envelope, an inch thick and less than a pound in weight. Still it contained the same capabilities as the original. This one, he said, had appeared *two* years ago.

Emphasizing the need for ongoing research and development, he then held between his thumb and forefinger an object so small it could barely be seen by us in the audience. No larger than a dollar and weighing approximately four ounces, this was today's model of the eight-year-old, sixteen-pound computer, bearing within itself the phenomenal mentality and operational potential of its cumbersome, overweight original. As if this were not enough, the science educator let it be known that one of our leading electronic companies was currently producing a semi-conductor so infinitesimally small that a thousand of them could be placed on the head of a pin.

In the wake and glamour of this I was asked to speak, and it seemed to me an assignment as difficult as bringing an omnibus of space travelers back to Mother Earth. But one basic truth was recognized by all of us: the marvel of man's ingenuity is matched and outmatched by man himself. The mind that made the computer is greater than the computer that is made, just as the creator is greater than the object he creates.

The phenomenon of man

My listeners agreed that man, who has made so many fearful and wonderful things, is himself fearfully and wonderfully made. A moment of reflection persuaded us that even our obviously physical life is unrealized and unseen until we begin to examine it, until we are confronted by some of the fantastic and popular facts about ourselves. We are composed of 500 coordinated muscles, 200 bones, seven miles of nerve fibre, thirty feet of alimentary canal, and other things too numerous to mention—all synchronized and controlled by a computer—the brain—so small that it fits neatly into one's head, but which if it were constructed according to today's electronic systems would require a five-story building. Besides all of which, this intricate apparatus called man is sustained by a tiny pump, the heart, a soft and hollow organ weighing no more than ten or twelve ounces, but propelling seventy-five gallons of blood per hour, day after day, at some seventy thrusts a minute, 36,000,-000 times a year for an average of seventy years. Furthermore, the entire complicated mechanism works while we sleep, resting only between beats, rebuilding, restoring, rejuvenating us so that with a bit of care and common sense it requires amazingly little over-hauling, correction, or repair. Great was the power of reflection when we turned the electronic microscope upon ourselves!

Would we ever be able to look into the "source of life" as had been suggested? Was research in the "inner man" keeping pace with the exploits in outer space, and were we prepared for the adventure in exploring our deeper self?

Who could say?

I recalled my visit to Rome during the opening sessions of the Ecumenical Council. I felt, as did many others, that the man who was most instrumental in influencing the proceedings was one who wasn't there. In fact, he had died broken-hearted and alone in New York in 1955. His name: Pierre Teilhard de Chardin. His place in the Church: a Jesuit with the thorough, fluent training of a skilled paleontologist. The reason for his influence: he had written boldly about the origin and nature of man in terms more scien-tific than theological. With infinite insight and dedicated will, he had proposed that human life had evolved through countless eons and that it is still evolving, seeking to reach a conceivable but perhaps unattainable goal, suggesting that the individual goes through the cycles of aspiration and growth which are reflected in the rise and fall of cultures. For years the Church rejected Chardin's theories and ordered him silenced, but now as the white-robed delegates gathered to re-examine truth under the brilliant light of a nuclear-conscious age, the spirit of Pierre was there, projecting new insights and reflections on the screen of thought.

I imagined that he was watching the proceedings from some special vantage point in the spirit realm.

Chardin believed that the supreme moment in life's evolvement was that instant when, for the first time in a living creature, "instinct perceived itself in its own mirror."

"Within the crisis of reflection," he said, "the next turn in the drama manifests itself. Psychogenesis which led to man now effaces itself, relieved or absorbed by another and a higher function—the engendering and development of all the stages of the mind." To this process he gave the grand-sounding term *noogenesis* and reminded us that each time a richer and more highly developed life appears it is the result of a correspondingly highly developed consciousness, the result of reflection on the limitless potential within each and every one of us.

Now the modern fathers of the Church sat in conference in the massive and overpowering atmosphere of St. Peter's. Robed in ecclesiastical garb reminiscent of the changeless tradition of faith, surrounded by the medieval grandeur of inspired art unmatched and unchanging, they were confronted by the projected image cast by one of their own confrères on the Church's historic screen. Where *did* human life originate and how *did* man evolve?

They opened Chardin's book, *The Phenomenon of Man*, and heard him say, "Life, being an ascent of consciousness, cannot continue to advance without transforming itself in depth. Like all growing magnitudes in the world life has to become different so as to remain itself. Here, in accession to the power of reflection, emerges the particular and critical form of transformation. . . ."

When I read these words I found them an echo of something deep and responsive within my heart, conveying something I had always felt rather than understood, an insight and an awareness beyond my comprehension, but powerful enough to start me on a search for their ultimate meaning. There *is* an impulse within us which urges us on. Life must change in order to remain itself. We *cannot* truly advance unless we catch a vision of the unseen.

The impulse to ascend

Among the books my father handed down to me was one titled *The Book of Fate and Fortune.* It was filled with graphic formulas on all sorts of things: psalmistry, astrology, graphology, spiritualism. It put the big word "oniromancy" into my vocabulary and it never left me: oniromancy, the art and science of seeing the unseen projected on the screen of dreams. But most of all the old book impressed upon me the fact that each time a superior class of life is born, it is the result of a *desire on the part of life to ascend.*

The fishes, said the book, were born from the desire of some of the lower crustaceans to rid themselves of their hard shell and to live the free life of the oceans. The reptiles evolved from the desire of certain fish to leave the water and explore the land! The small mammals and birds were born from the desire of ambitious reptiles who wanted to walk and fly instead of continuing to crawl on their stomachs. Higher mammals resulted from the desire of the lower mammals to evolve, and human beings resulted from the desire of the more developed mammals to think and act on an ever higher plane. Evolution and growth, said *The Book of Fate and Fortune,* are not a matter of biological function, but rather the result of an innate impulse on the part of life to ascend. As the being recognizes more and more the inferiority of its present state, it longs for a higher and nobler environment and wherever the desire is sufficiently strong and sincere, the change takes place.

Not until I read Chardin's *Phenomenon* did I really believe in this kind of speculation. Not until he caught and held for a little while the moment when "instinct turns the mirror of reflection upon itself" did I find the feeling of the truth of it within myself. A desire to see the unseen and to ascend to it in experience seemed to me a great revelation; enough to make me wonder whether death itself might be just another step forward, an impulse on the part of some deeper self to evolve into a higher and greater world.

An enzyme invisible on its sliver of glass, a speck of a spider sliding down its unseen thread, a peanut in a wrinkled palm, a mustard seed in the Master's hand, a computer the size of a dollar, the Church fathers seated in St. Peter's basilica. . . .

The scientist switched on the laboratory lights as if to bring me back to reality.

"The secret of life," he said, "will not be found in outer space, but, rather, in this." His hand rested confidently on the microscope of which he was justly proud.

"Or in a mirror," I had to say, "during a moment of reflection on the mystery of self."

III ✦ AWARENESS

An unforgettable feature of the New York World's Fair was a film in the Kodak pavilion titled, *The Searching Eye*. Through the months of fair time, viewers filled the auditorium, captivated by the beauty and mystique of a simple story: a boy explores nature and the sea, builds his castles on the beach, finds a world of wonder in the shifting sands, and projects his dreams into the vastness of the rolling tide. For thirty enchanted minutes, people of all ages and every conceivable walk of life sat entranced in the pavilion theater, often remaining in thoughtful silence after the picture had ended.

Evidently each spectator saw within himself the world as he visualized it through the marvel of his own searching eye, for we all have built our castles of sand and watched the sea, and wondered at the power of nature as it challenged our control. But most of all, we were stirred by the reminder that our hopes and ideals are never really destroyed, never actually washed away so far as our dreams are concerned. Something keeps telling us that the spirit behind the castle-building is the *real* and is considerably more lasting than the castles that are built.

Such was the secret of *The Searching Eye* and such is the message of many intriguing films which reflect what our innermost self recognizes as the enduring and meaningful elements of life. Movies of this kind interpret life as we have idealized it, as if to assure us that the world fabled in our creative thoughts must exist somewhere even as it has been projected to the magic of the big screen.

Disney pictures, for example, awaken the unseen by presenting characters as we imagine them to be and as we want them to be in keeping with our deepest wish. Through skilled artists and film technicians our hero is romanticized, whether it be a man like Johnny Appleseed or a mouse like Mickey. When his planting days are over, Johnny Appleseed is wafted to an apple-blossomed heaven just as we would have decreed. The mouse wins every encounter as we want him to do. Situations, too, receive the fairy touch. In *Mary Poppins*, for example, our innate longing was once more satisfied when we met exactly the kind of nanny we all longed for in our youth. For a little while, "God's in His heaven and all's right with the world."

Our golden dreams

This millennialistic hope has been man's quest since time began. Through myths and fables, parables and prophecies, our golden dreams have been sustained. Long years ago the writer of the Book of Revelation sketched it on a classical scale when, banished to the Isle of Patmos—a place intended only for exile and defeat—John made the most of his destiny and foresaw the peaceable kingdom where "the wolf shall dwell with the lamb, the leopard shall lie down with the kid; the calf and young lion and the fatling shall stand together, and a little child shall lead them."

The Peaceable Kingdom. Humanity's everlasting utopian ideal. Now we can understand why an itinerant Pennsylvania artist, Edward Hicks, made the subject of utopia his lifelong work and gave it an American twist. Wherever he traveled in early nineteenth-century America this talented Quaker painted his version of the perfect world, subtly inserting the historical incident of William Penn's "Holy Experiment" into a corner of his Kingdom masterpieces. Over and over he painted the scenes, then gave the canvases to friends who saw in them what we, in our modern day, saw and felt in *The Searching Eye.*

But how can we have and hold this kind of world when the

cold facts bring us back to earth and warn us that we may merely have been hypnotized by theatrical illusion and bewitched by artistic skill? Out of the theater, back again in the traffic and tempo of the times, it is easy to conclude that the moments in front of the big screen were but fantasy and not really real. Must the good life, we wonder, always be but make-believe and escape, with reality never quite fitting the dream? Must the castles we hopefully build always be swept away by the tides?

An answer to the questions came to me when I pieced together some of the fragments of my own boyhood, turning a searching eye upon myself. There was a cousin of mine in our relationship with the grand-sounding title: *Herr Doktor Paulus*. German-trained, with a Ph.D. in philosophy, and a sabre wound under his left eye—a proud memento of a duel in a Berlin *Gymnasium*—he boasted of his acquaintance with Freud and Jung and Kraepelin long before psychoanalysis became a conversation piece.

My brothers and I dreaded Cousin Paul's visits, for *Herr Doktor* had a way of changing the house into a classroom. However, he also had a facility for bringing things down to the level of common sense whenever he was in the mood, and it was out of one of these moods that he offered a suggestion about the perplexing dilemma, "How can we have the kind of world we would like to have?"

His answer was definite, "Take an inventory of the kind of a world you've got!"

He illustrated his point one evening when my father, mother, and the four of us children sat together in the living room of our home. It was then that *Herr Doktor Paulus* announced we would play a game to which he had given the intriguing name of *Katzenspiel—Cat's Play.*

Ordering us to close our eyes, he said, "Now while your eyes are shut, I want each of you to describe the room we are in. What are the walls like? What color are the carpets? Give me the titles of the books. Tell me the pattern of the curtains. Explain what is on the mantel. Tell me everything you know about these surroundings. Kant once said that the eye is impotent without the mind. Now let us discover what the mind is like without the eye!"

Needling and prodding, he shamed us into the realization that the house we lived in was filled with details and treasures we had never noticed or else forgotten. "What!" he exclaimed. "You do not know how many lights are in the chandelier or how many figurines on the fireplace? You cannot tell me if the door opens in or out even though you go through it every day? You cannot even describe the chair you are sitting in?"

Take inventory of your blessings

Cat's Play. A cat, Cousin Paul avowed, can see in the dark, but we unobservant mortals refuse to see and remember our surroundings even in the light. So he commanded us to open our eyes, proud that he had humbled us with his *Katzenspiel,* and confident that he had made his meaning clear: we fail to see our blessings, just as we neglect the hidden scenes we live with day by day. They are here, but we refuse to see them. He concluded that if we do not appreciate what we have, we can never be trusted with the things we want, but if we fairly appraise our life we realize we already possess many of the things we desire. And this, he felt, applied not only to material things but to our philosophies and beliefs as well.

The world I lived in during those years before the years of maturity began was a compact, fenced-in world, slower in tempo and different in values than the world today. Many of the simple convictions I believed in are now irreclaimably gone and most of the dogmatic beliefs I grew up with are as outmoded as the game we played. But something of the spirit of the playing keeps returning and asks with quiet certitude, "What do you see?"

What do you see as the aim of life and as the goals that bring contentment? What do you see when you seriously consider your place in the scheme of things or when you visualize occasions that bring true happiness and delight? "Take an inventory!" And gradually I came to realize that life is the room we live in, life is the things we live with, life is the door opening in or out.

The art of awareness

But it was not only through his *Cat's Play* that *Herr Paulus* taught me to appreciate the nature of existence. With merciless pedagogy, he pounded another German jaw-breaker into my consciousness: *Gewahrsamkeit,* the art of being aware. Today the word is not so startling, since philosophers have regaled us with terms such as "is-ness," "wasness," "suchness," "*Ding an Sich*" (the thing in itself), and others which often complicate simple truths. In the light of these, *Gewahrsamkeit* is quite in order, especially since *Herr Doktor* assured me it held out considerable promise of reward.

The art of awareness, he contended, represents that impulse in man's nature which teaches the body how to live, the spirit how to love, and the mind how to assimilate the thoughts that come to it.

Awareness reminds us that we grow by way of difficulties and by facing reality fully as much as we do through the nostalgia of the big screen. We develop not only by having our ideals confirmed but by having our opinions challenged. Meaning and strength are imparted to us when the sea rubs out our castles of sand no less than when we hold back the tide in theatrical make-believe. Struggle and encounter are the cutting edges of growth and we should, by rights, be grateful that the world outside the theater forces us to face this fact.

Life is *being.* It is not *a* being, it is being itself. We may say, "Today I am not up to par, I am not myself," or affirm that, "Today I am really on top of the world," but the truth is that life is life. It is every moment and every day. It is every feeling and every encounter, every note in the scale, every wave in the spectrum, every arc in the circle of experience, and awareness helps provide the means to take all of life in stride.

Some say it was awareness that caused a President, John F. Kennedy, to quote a verse from Shakespeare before his martyrdom,

> "The sun's o'ercast with blood:
> Fair day, adieu!
> Which is the side that I must go
> Withal?

I am with both; each army hath
a hand,
And in their rage, I having hold
of both,
They whirl asunder and dismember me."

Awareness inspired a mystic, Meister Eckhart to proclaim, "The seed of God is in us and it will thrive and grow. Pear seeds grow into pear trees, nut seeds into nut trees, and God seed into God."

Awareness as a life-changing force persuaded an alcoholic, "Dr. Bill," founder of the AA movement, to face himself and say, "It is only a matter of being willing to believe in a power greater than myself. Nothing more is required of me to make my beginning. . . . At last a new world comes into view."

Awareness caused actor John Payne to recall a prayer of faith as he lay critically injured on a New York street, the victim of a careening car, "The light of God surrounds me, the love of God enfolds me, the power of God protects me, the presence of God watches over me. Wherever I am, God is!"

Awareness prompted a religious leader, Frank B. Robinson, to reply to those who predicted he would die during the night, "Nothing doing! I will live until I have accomplished what I set out to do."

Awareness revealed to writer James Weldon Johnson how death came to a loved one, "While we were watching round her bed, she saw what we did not see. She saw old death. But death didn't frighten Sister Caroline. He looked to her like a welcome friend . . . and she closed her eyes and said, 'I'm going home.'"

Awareness spoke through R. H. Grenville when she said,

"Oh, let my eyes be opened wide,
That I may clearly see,
How often in another's guise,
God walks the road with me."

Awareness caused a pragmatist, William James, to take a philosophically humorous look at life and to conclude, "This old universe will never be completely good as long as one being is unhappy, or as long as one poor cockroach suffers the pangs of unrequited love!"

"Through the art of being aware," Doctor Paul maintained, "you can change the novice to a genius, the sinner into a saint, and endow the blind with inner sight."

Gewahrsamkeit. The word came back to me, spun from the spell of *The Searching Eye.*

It came back to me at other times and in other places. I thought of it while riding through the Blue Ridge Mountains with industrialist Shirley Mitchell. Here was the president and boss of one of America's largest freight lines with an uncanny ability to see the commonly unseen. An extraordinary awareness was reflected not only in his big and booming business, which keeps some 2000 freight trucks rolling night and day, but in his avocation and his hobbies which have to do with preserving early American traditions.

Great vision and childlike trust

I realized again that men who do great things combine great visions with an almost childlike trust and wonder about life's inexhaustible possibilities. They seem to live in two worlds at once, the world of traffic and time, and the timeless world of the big screen—and to them these worlds are one.

I caught on to this during frequent trips with Mr. Mitchell when he spied things out of the corner of his eye, things which ordinary men would hardly have noticed. Calling my attention to an old barn, a half-forgotten trail, a rambling rail fence or a hand-hewn house, he reconstructed history and tied these landmarks into the world of today, like Hicks painting his pictures of the *Peaceable Kingdom,* like a boy walking beside the sea, like a youngster playing *Katzenspiel.* From an appreciation of the misty haze of the Virginia mountains to the sight of a deserted parish church, he was aware of the vibrancy of life around him and caused a hidden world to unfold until I saw it, too.

One day we came upon a weather-beaten mill near a creek in the Meadows of Dan. Half-hidden behind the miller's house, it nestled against a wooded slope thick with a tangle of dogwood and oaks. To most people it would have been little more than a deserted symbol of the passing years. Mitchell saw in it the hope that someone would come along to open its doors and breathe life back into the mechanism that time had stilled.

I was not surprised when, later, I learned that he had dredged the creek bed, restored the rotted timbers, refurbished the screens and chutes and belts and bins so that the picturesque old mill was once more good as new, yet venerable with age as it should be. Soon it was back in operation, water-grinding meal for which there was suddenly a great demand, and recalling for today's generations the heritage of a quieter but nonetheless industrious past.

Life, as *Doktor Paulus* would say, is Mitchell's room. His genius for seeing what others overlook gives him the right to live in an exciting, challenging, never-static world. I learned from him that to accomplish great things we must combine awareness with activity, and to reach a given goal we must never lose the measure of our dreams. For it is one thing to be aware and quite another to do something with our awareness.

"Some people," as G. B. Shaw once said, "see things as they are and ask why. Others dream of things that never were and ask why not?" No matter in which classification we happen to fall, we all have our moments of awareness, moments in which we feel there are ideas yet to be expressed and we may express them, songs to be born which we may sing, books to be written which we may write, dreams in embryo, exploits to be undertaken, experiences to be lived, and adventures in the making in which we can play a part. Give some people awareness and the place in which they stand, wherever it may be, becomes for them the place for opportunity.

You would not expect much conversation to come from a Trappist monastery where the monks are rigorously pledged to perpetual silence. But from the stillness of Our Lady of Gethsemane in Kentucky, where I made my first retreat, a monk named Thomas Merton has provided help and direction to thousands of people through his inspired writings. He is read because he stresses an awakening of the awareness of the presence of God, believing as most thoughtful people do that man is religious by nature. And the reason monk Merton inspires awareness is because he practices the fine art of being aware.

The Singing Nun

Consider the impact made within the past few years by *Soeur Sourire.* Here was a girl very much like, and very much unlike, other girls in their early twenties. One day she bought an ordinary guitar that hung by its neck in an old shop window in Brussels. A few coins, the last she had, bought it. She tucked it under her arm and made her way to Fichermont and to the convent of the Dominican order. Her prayer was simple, "Dear God, make something worth-while of my life." Her question to a rose as she bent over it in the convent garden was sincere, "Who knows what you and my guitar and I might do together?"

During her novitiate groups of young girls came frequently to the convent for retreats. Evenings after the hours of work and worship, the Singing Nun and her guitar sang about the rose and the sea and the stars and the rendezvous with *le Seigneur;* songs of the searching-seeing type, filled with an awareness of the everlasting quest. In soft, feeling-full tones she sang,

> "I found the Lord on the beach,
> I found the Lord in a white seashell.
>
> I found the Lord in the breeze,
> I found the Lord in the intoxicating wind.
>
> I found the Lord within the mist,
> I found the Lord on the dew-covered dunes.
>
> Little boat upon the water,
> Float, float,
> Little boat upon the water,
> Float, my soul,
> Toward the Most High."

Caught in the spell of the winsome voice of *Soeur Sourire,* the retreatants begged permission to take both songs and voice home with them so they could hear these quaint chansons in the work-aday world. The Mother Superior gave her permission and several recordings were made in a Brussels' studio. So began the romance of the Singing Nun and the great wide world. Wherever people heard the songs they wanted them. They said it made them aware of a gentleness and a response in their own hearts, and that the music caused them to reflect more deeply on the meaning of life. Today, go where you will, you can hear the voice of *Soeur Sourire*, especially as she sings the secret song of everyman,

"Dominic, oh Dominic,
Over the land he plods along
And sings a little song,
Never looking for reward,
He just talks about the Lord.

Grant us now, oh Dominic,
The grace of love and simple mirth,
That we all may help to quicken,
Godly love and truth on earth."

The art of being aware.

We develop it by reflection; by seeing, through thought, the commonly unseen.

We discover it by association with those who have eyes to see, those to whom it is immaterial whether the object seen is real or merely the hopeful projection of an ideal.

We improve it by daring to be fascinated with the childhood wonders of the searching eye, wonders which mystic minds have always found intriguing:

"To see the world in a grain of sand,
And heaven in a wild flower;
Hold infinity in the palm of your hand
And Eternity in an hour."

We identify ourselves with it by finding lessons of life wherever we go, in whatever we do, and wherever we are—lessons of awareness in such simple things as a rose in a garden or lilies in the field, or by daring to conclude from the wonder of little children that "theirs is the kingdom of heaven."

The island doctor

A practical demonstration of how awareness works was impressed upon me by a college student in Seoul, Korea. This young man, Rhee Yil Sun, had written for permission to translate one of my books into his native language. References in the book to Dr. Albert Schweitzer had especially intrigued him, and someday he thought he might write something about the jungle doctor of Lambarene.

Permission for Rhee to translate my book was given and some months later a Korean copy arrived, along with a note from the translator, "The life and work of Albert Schweitzer have filled me with an *awareness of the challenge of my own life*. The question now is what I must do about myself and my own medical career." He thought perhaps he was being "called" to become a doctor of the Schweitzer type.

The following year, while I was in Rangoon, I met Rhee Yil Sun and found him to be a deeply committed, serious-minded medic ready for his internship. He reported that he was on his way to Africa to visit the man who had made him aware of his mission in life. Dr. Schweitzer had indicated he would be glad to see him.

I followed Rhee's story closely after that, followed it through his stay at Lambarene and his unselfish service in the leper village and the hospital. I learned that while he was in Lambarene, the legendary Schweitzer baptized him in the Christian faith and christened him with a new name, Timothy Rhee.

Recently I was informed that Dr. Rhee, having returned to Korea, gave up an opportunity for a medical practice in Seoul and went instead to a lonely, rugged isle, Ullung-Do, in the eastern sea. Here as the only doctor on an island of 20,000 people he set up his medical ministry. "I see my dream unfolding," he wrote me. "We are now serving sixty-five leprosy patients, 150 victims of T.B., and the hundreds who need preventive vaccine. Assistants are beginning to come to Ullung-Do in the spirit in which I came. With our good results in restoring health, the islanders' trust in us is growing."

The world will hear more of this island doctor. He will be written about and talked about and a movie will be made of him, as it was of Schweitzer, and of Tom Dooley, and of Dr. Gordon Seagrave in Burma, and as one will be made of Larry Mellon in Haiti and of the late Paul Carlson in the Congo. The secret of the call to Rhee and others lies in a single word: awareness, of the kind that recognizes that where our talent meets the need of the world, that is where God wants us to be.

And what do you see when you look at a *rock?*

I stopped one day along a highway in Montana because I had caught sight of a wisp of a man building a wall. Here he was, a hunchbacked laborer on his knees constructing one of the most artistic dry rock walls I had ever seen, a wall designed to serve a dual purpose, that of beautifying the entrance to a lane leading to a ranch, and holding back erosion caused by seepage from a spring.

When I told him that projects of this kind were something of a hobby with me, he said he liked this sort of work because each stone offered a challenge: it had a place where it would fit, the trick was to find the place. He had handpicked the stones and hauled them here. He wiped them clean and sorted them into groups which he called regulars, irregulars, crooks, misfits, ornery cusses, and so on. In its proper place, however, the ornery cuss was just as important as a regular. He handled each with affection. He did not use cement, he said, because it seemed to him that any kind of stickum defaced the natural quality of the stones and, he allowed, would probably make them feel that they were locked in a prison instead of living in a wall.

The real reward

When I commented enthusiastically on his work, he replied with just three words, "Is that so?" and the way he said it made it the most wonderful of answers. It was a question, but as affirmative as any positive statement could possibly have been. The words seemed to say, "It is good of you to appreciate my work, for a man likes to feel he has done well with a job. But it really does not matter, you know, what you or anyone thinks. Cars pass here all day, but very few stop, which may be as it should be, for, after all, only he who touches the stones and places them where they fit can really understand the joy of work."

To all of which I wanted to reply with his own words, "Is that so?" For it occurred to me as it must have to him that there is actually not much virtue in work unless one finds a reward in it beyond the reward of being paid for the job, important as the dollars may be. Just to work, anyone can do that. Even people in captive countries do that. But to a free man work is a way of life, a complement to awareness and a pathway to a goal.

Cat's Play and *The Searching Eye.* Caught between thoughts of the past and present and casting a glance toward the future, I found myself taking an inventory and asking myself, "How does the room you live in look to you?"

My room. My room called life. It was a good room with plenty of windows, you might say, looking out over the world, and plenty of doors admitting to the work and ways of people everywhere.

Sometimes it seemed a bit too comfortable, this room of mine, and an awareness crept in that it should be filled with more service to mankind and greater contributions to the needs and problems of the modern world. But most of all, when I looked at my room of life, I saw two fundamental awarenesses: appreciation for things at hand and guidance for things to come. The two were inexorably joined. *The more I am grateful, the more I am guided.*

Once more I sat with closed eyes recalling the details and treasures of my surroundings, taking an inventory, and asking myself, "What do you see?"

Once more I faced the overriding art of awareness on the level of a boy on the beach with his castles of sand and his look of wonder as the tide swept in. Whether on the big screen or on the teeming street, the worlds are real and indivisible.

Cat's Play.

The Searching Eye.

There is no sound or sight that awareness does not deepen, no experience that it will not enrich, no adventure that it will not heighten, and no conflict that it will not help resolve.

Perhaps there is no dream that it will not eventually bring to life.

IV * PERCEPTION

We were flying at 100 miles an hour some 250 feet above the majestic Selkirk range in British Columbia. In the tail of our Cessna was a strange and intricate mechanism connected with a maze of cabin instrumentation that left only cramped room for our plane's three occupants. We were contour flying over meadows draped on mountain slopes and we were buzzing across rugged outcroppings of blue-green rock.

The crew of the plane—pilot and technician—were interested in other things besides the thrill of flying. So was I. Precious metals, for example, and rare earth of the kind spied out by aero survey planes such as ours.

The instrument in the tail was a magnetometer similar to the one that figured in the fabulous Timmins find in Ontario where some 60,000,000 tons of silver, copper, and zinc were detected by these electronic prospectors-in-the-sky. By recording magnetic attraction and electrical conductivity in the earth's magnetic field, this uncanny device combed the land in search of mother lode.

I knew this country. I had spent my summers here for nearly twenty years. I was familiar with every curve in the twisting road that hugged the hillsides along the lake. I had climbed many of the mountain peaks, had searched for hidden springs and fished the coves and sandy points of this enchanting ninety-mile-long stretch of shimmering blue. I loved every inch of this Kootenay country but now I was seeing it in a new perspective and appreciating it even more. Through the marvel of modern instrumentation we were rolling back the age-old curtain of Mother Earth and sorting through her treasures which no one had ever seen.

Perception!

The thrill for me was in the wonder of it, for I thought of the days of the sourdoughs, the prospector with his pick and shovel, the gold hound with his old tin pan, the grubstaker with his sticks of dynamite, wearing out heart and hand in the granite jungle of the Kootenay. Here we were, comfortable in our bucket seats on a crystal clear day, soaring in seagull style over the billowy expanse of mountains and lake below. Nothing to do but fly over beach and crag, read the instruments, and later key the computed records with aerial maps, pinpointing the possible finds.

What do you see when you look at a plane? The average observer glancing up at us would hardly have suspected that we were equipped to see the commonly unseen, to penetrate through brush and stone and search out veins and treasures hidden from normal sight.

A *treasure in every mine*

The flight became a lesson in perception. Obviously, no matter where or at what period in history man appears on the scene, the resources he needs are always there according to his ability to perceive them. This was hinted at as we crossed and recrossed an old mine site nestling neglected among the encroaching forest. Years ago this grubbed-out pit had been a profitable producer of lead and zinc. When these were exhausted it was abandoned for many years until a new metal, tungsten, was needed in the life of man.

When the tungsten search began, the deposits and waste of the old excavation were reassayed, and suddenly the ghost mine sprang back into activity. It offered up enough of the precious ore to support a thriving settlement, causing it to continue on its own long after the tungsten had run out. Now here we were, probing the old mine again, and the instruments were registering as if to assure us that other treasures were waiting now that man was once more on the hunt for something new. The incident confirmed in no uncertain terms the fact that, as far as a mine is concerned, it is never totally exhausted. It is merely a matter of discovering what can be done with that which is newly found.

This was consoling for me, for when we flew over Coffee Creek in the Ainsworth area I recalled having invested in some stock in a prospector's venture in the gaping slopes below. I bought the shares mainly because the mine had a good name, "Old Jerusalem." Old Jerusalem near Coffee Creek. What could go wrong with a name like that? It was a good name, but a worthless mine, and I decided that in the future I might do better in a good mine with a worthless name. Nonetheless, the magnetometer was lustily jotting its findings on the profile recorder, and who could say that Old Jerusalem would not pay off eventually? At least it was a thought and filled me with the will to believe that treasures are always awaiting the persistent prospector in his time.

"What's left for me?"

Was it not equally true to assume that what God did with the earth —packed it with riches to be discovered according to their need— He also did with life?

I had always been slow in accepting this theory. I grew up with the opinion that talents run out, as time does. Life's mine, I contended, could be mined dry, leaving its owner in despair. Not so. A new perception told me we have treasures for every age and every period. We need but *perceive* them and remember that, as a protection against our own dissipation, some are held for us in trust.

I once had the mistaken idea that God's riches, like the coins of all realms, were measurable and limited. They were like grain in a bin and there was just so much to go around. More than that, I had been given a scoop of a certain size, and mine was just big enough or small enough to help get me by in a highly competitive world. Not so. It is a matter of perception.

I also had the mistaken idea that time is a straight line. It isn't. It is an ever-widening contour circle. I thought that history had a beginning and would, therefore, have an end and that my fortune was determined by the point in history where I appeared on the scene. I learned that the determining factor is where we are in our state of perception and this depends upon the forces we attract to ourselves in the magnetic field of life which knows no beginning and no end.

When my pastor uncle died and the bells tolled out the long years of his covenant with the Lord, my eight-year-old-heart called to me to enter the ministry someday. Then and there, however, my childish mind warned me that by the time I grew up and was ordained, all the people in the world would already have been "saved" and religion's mission would long since have been finished and fulfilled.

One look at the world today convinces me that nothing is ever actually finished, and I do not mean in religion only. In every nook and niche of life, from the latest medical breakthrough to the next discovery in outer space, nothing is ever final or fixed or as yet perfectly fulfilled, and in this fact may lie life's greatest meaning.

The answer to the nagging question, "What's left for me?" is "Everything!" Wherever you stand in the "time arc," at whatever age and in whatever place, is the center of things.

We adjust better to science than we do to philosophy. Most of us these days believe in science more than we do in religion. We believe in technological miracles. We just *know* that the worlds "out there" will be conquered and eventually inhabited by earth's people. Planets beyond the known planets and universes beyond our own do not appall us. We are persuaded that we can master any and all worlds that float in the ocean of space.

Where perception weakens is in the estimate of our ability to control our inner world and to perform the necessary spiritual miracles. Fear that we lack the capacity to rule ourselves or to be trusted with the liberties and the luxuries of life, no less than with our rising responsibilities, haunts us; haunts us only because we forget that the treasury of ideas is inexhaustible and that new approaches to complexities, like the discoveries of new metals, merely await the magnetometer of the mind and the soul.

It was natural to think these thoughts from "on high" in a survey plane. It was easy to conclude under the thrill of flying that we should always find solutions to problems, not escape from them, and to remember that the mountains in life often produce the richest discoveries. Perception is the secret, the necessary key for unlocking the inner riches. It tells us that if we must frequently accept the commonplace we will find that it hides the uncommon, just as is the case with uncommon minerals locked in the common terrain.

All this was simple during flight, but what would I do with this philosophizing when I got back to earth? A person should always try to look at life from above. Maybe this is what is meant by staying "on top of things." What do you see when you look at a mountain? Beauty, romance, adventure, the challenge to climb, the thrill of conquering the peak, but from above I saw the unlimited potentials yet to be revealed through the magic eye of perception.

The foreordained fortunes

What do you see when you look at your home from the sky, especially when a magnetometer is sailing like a meteor over the house? We were crossing the summer cabin which my wife and I had built on Destiny Bay years ago. For the moment it did not matter what the detector instruments were registering. The "mine" over which we were passing was pure gold. The gray shakes of the cabin roof, the bluestone patio, the winding lane, the guest house, the breakwater, the hillsides—all persuaded me that everyone should by rights see his residence from a survey plane so that he would once more measure his treasures.

Most cabins, I imagine, began as ours did, not with architectural drawings, but with a dream. There were no buildings on this hillside when Lorena and I first visited it. There were only the magnificent trees—fir, cedar, and maples—protectively enclosing the grassy slope which extended down to the water's edge. We had admired the place many times and once I asked Lorena why she thought no one had ever built a home on this attractive site. Her answer was all I needed to inquire about eventual ownership. She said, "Maybe it has been waiting for us."

That, it seemed to me, was a remarkable remark. Perhaps there *are* things in life waiting just for us, for you, for everyone. That, too, may be part of a divine conspiracy in the thrilling adventure of life. Just as there is a specific personality and a certain niche in time which are uniquely ours and unlike that of any other, just so there may also be predestined things needing only our perceptive will to detect and claim them. I had always felt that Destiny Bay was one of these foreordained fortunes and now as I looked down from the air, my belief was reaffirmed.

I asked the pilot to circle the grounds again. After all, this was treasure. This was what perception had drawn out of the unseen when I first sketched the design for the cabin on a piece of discarded wrapping paper, left by picnickers in the trampled grass. This was how our Destiny Bay "mine" was staked. This was part of my early prospecting of the pick-and-shovel type, and who was to say that the grubstaker was not quite content to wear out his heart and hand in the granite jungle, or to give back the vision of goodness to that which had filled him with the dream.

So we ended our survey flight and it seemed to me that the gods of chance and fate, of hunches and guidance and superstition which early sourdoughs followed had now been confirmed electronically. The words of an old professor of mine came to mind, "We are moving toward the day when in scientific guise we see what early man saw through his masks: there is no time, only eternity; there is no space, only infinity."

Adventures with "mood-making" drugs

The perception that the mines of the inner life are fully as inexhaustible as the mines in nature prompted some fascinating research in the subjective field of human experience. Here, in "inner space," the role of the magnetometer was played by fantasy-forming drugs called psychedelics or hallucinogens. A flight into this area, I was told, would hold exciting discoveries, and a number of my friends had for some years been prospecting in these fields. They referred to psychedelics as consciousness-expanding, soul-probing, wonder-working agents, among which the major ones were LSD, mescaline and psilocybin.

Psychotropic drugs such as hashish and soma were old as the hills, but now it was claimed there were new instruments of perceptivity ready to trigger a radically awakened sense of the inner life. Little was said about the dangers or the highly deleterious effect of these encounters and wherever I went on college campuses students asked me my reaction to this approach to perceptivity.

Gerald Heard, whose friendship I cherished and whose all too frequent psychedelic trips I often wondered about, speculated that, "Here may be a major breakthrough that meets the problem of letting in a free flow of comprehension beyond the everyday threshold of experience . . . and this seems to be accomplished by confronting one's self, a standing outside one's self, a dissolution of the ego-based apprehensions that cloud the sky of the mind."

Aldous Huxley, with whom I had planned to take mescaline before his untimely death, described his impressions in his book *The Doors of Perception* and maintained that mescaline could produce a "transcendental experience" which will leave the participant "wiser but less cocksure, happier but less self-satisfied, humbled in acknowledging his ignorance yet better equipped to understand the relationship of words to things, of systematic reasoning to the unfathomable mystery which tries, forever vainly, to comprehend."

Dr. John Aiken, an osteopath of Socorro, New Mexico, proclaimed psychedelics worthy of being sacramentalized and was prepared to administer them in a spiritual setting as a new and modern eucharist.

These and other respected friends issued such exotic reports that when I asked one of them what he saw when he looked at a rose while under the influence of mescaline, he said, "I saw the petals fold and unfold. It was a living, moving organism. I saw the shades melt into a multi-colored stream. The heart of the rose was pure gold and in the center I saw God."

Yet through all the welter of claims to which the high priest of psychedelics, Dr. Timothy Leary, added his euphoric testimonies, there were increasing medical reports about the brain-damaging effects of this kind of chemical experimentation. Laboratory researchers warned that chronic users of psychedelics showed psychiatric disorders ranging from mild anxiety to serious psychiatric abnormalities.

I gave the matter a great deal of thought. For thousands of years, individuals had sought enlightenment through various disciplines such as prayer and fasting, sacrifices and self-abnegation. Often they sought an expanding consciousness and beatific visions through long periods of mystical contemplation. Now we were asked to believe that the same kind of transformation could be effected instantly through a tongue touch of LSD (lysergic acid diethylamide) or other innovative hallucinogens. By the very nature of my work and research I decided to discover for myself what my reaction would be to one of these short cuts to deepened perceptivity, if such there be.

Experiment with peyote

I opted to involve myself with one of the most common and no doubt the most lowly of the psychedelics, namely, peyote.

Surely, peyote *was* the most unsophisticated in the entire mood-making family, and it may have been this very fact that attracted me. It was more earthy and uncontrived than its offspring mescaline, more modest than psilocybin, and whereas LSD was of relatively recent origin, having been discovered serendipitously by a Swiss chemist in 1943, peyote had a history as old as drumbeats and had been used as a sacrament by the Native American (Indian) Church of America for a century or more.

One of my earliest introductions to peyotism had been by way of a book given me by Henry A. Wallace: *The Diabolic Root* written by Vincenzo Petrullo during WPA days. This firsthand account of peyote practices lured me into Delaware Indian country near Anadarko, Oklahoma, where the scene of Petrullo's stories was laid. Obscure rites are still conducted near Anadarko, but like religions which level off after the death of their leaders, so peyotism had lost much of its sacred fire.

One thing, however, had not changed, and that was peyote itself. I found it growing in flowerpots, faithfully tended. A species of the cactus (mescal), small, spineless, the tops are in the form of leathery buttons about the size of a silver dollar. The dried buttons are chewed or smoked or brewed into a tea when used in ritualistic sessions. The

Indians considered it a god and said, "Peyote always does what the Father tells Him to do."

What, I wondered, would it do for me?

A friend agreed to sit in on my peyote session as an observer. A physician, interested in psychedelics, acted as monitor. Ordinarily there are two or more participants in the actual experience, but, again, for personal reasons, I wanted to try it alone, preparing myself for this solo trip by inspirational readings and meditation on the night prior to the proposed Sunday morning session.

At 9 A.M. I chewed and ate the grated peyote button and a vile tasting one it was. It lingered in my mouth like sour yeast. I had been told there would be a feeling of nausea and there was. I was also prepared for the accompanying chills and the sense of ominous foreboding which others had assured me was part of the process. I thought then how silly it was to take any kind of an oral agent for the sake of feeling sick when what I was after was spiritual perception. Not until the last rancid kernel had been swallowed did I turn my attention to the soft sound of religious recordings and some readings from *The Prophet*.

An hour passed and there were gradual reactions, suggestions that my sight was sharpened and my hearing more acute, but I assumed these might be mere imaginings, wishful thinking that something phenomenal would actually come from all this.

Another half hour and a sense of something arresting and spiritually intensive crept over me. Time became unimportant. I was wrapped in a cloud of self-perception obviously unreal but tantalizing, a feeling that everything I had ever set out to accomplish in life *had* been accomplished in a fantastically real and wonderful way and that now, as I perceived this, every sense of limitation and frustration left me. In its place loomed a growing sense of grand fulfillment. Thoughts I had often wanted to express but which had eluded me, talents which had been thwarted, the full and complete expression of who and what I considered myself to be in the inner core of my being, all these were now seemingly realized, not in these moments only, but retroactively in all time. For once in my life I knew that wherever I felt I had failed, I had actually succeeded!

My early musical career which had not amounted to much suddenly crystalized in virtuosity. A recording by Isaac Stern which was spinning gayly on the record player filled me with absolute assurance that *my* violin playing had thoroughly outclassed his and had been better received by my bygone listeners than his could ever be! When my friend read a portion of *The Prophet,* I was convinced that my writings were superior to Kahlil Gibran's! For once in my life I knew beyond the shadow of doubt that the best in me had been expressed through a clear channel for that expression. No need feeling that I had not achieved, because I unquestionably had!

That was the gist of it. Before the drug wore off, however, in early afternoon, I had a dark cavernous experience in which I was taunted by the illusion of my pride, and when I emerged from this theater of my inner self, laughing and crying and shaking my head at the incongruity of it all, I felt alone and sad, hopelessly unfulfilled.

Did this experience effect a change in my life? No more than the flight in the survey plane changed my thoughts about flying. Let's say that the experience was quickly homogenized in life's total overview, and that the recollection of my few enchanted moments only made me more aware than ever that I had not yet expressed my hidden best and perhaps I never would. There was a disturbing reaction about all this. What, I wondered, is the difference between an attempt at chemicalized perception and a similar "trip" on alcohol or marijuana or any other unpredictable drug? True, the setting, the dosage, one's attitude and one's whole libido are involved here, but how do we reconcile an outer mechanism of any kind with a true inner discovery?

Despite their romancing about psychedelics, none of my friends who indulged in them ever laid claim to what mystics would call heightened awareness or cosmic consciousness, and few felt that their creativity was sharpened because of their flights into the nether-nether land of the hallucinogens. They did insist, however, that they were more sensitized in their relationship with the total nature of existence, feeling themselves surrounded by a world substantially greater and more intimate than they had known before.

But isn't this something one can acquire almost instantly through quiet introspection? Isn't the first great step in perceptivity the knowledge that we already possess the capacity of uncommon perceiving and do not need a drug to tell us that? Isn't it better to realize that the spirit lives in us than to assume that through some chemical process we can be induced to live momentarily in the spirit?

At any rate, cumulative evidence continued to affirm that LSD users and chronic drug takers show a disturbing number of imminent dangers, cells with broken chromosomes, psychiatric disturbances, that women who are on LSD before and during pregnancy show an alarmingly high percentage of defective children, and that more and more congenital defects show injuries to the brain and the spinal column. In all of which I perceive there must be a better way to increase the power of perception than to take a chance on mood-making drugs or even the sacrament called peyote.

Our innate faculties of perception

There are other perceptions which may be realized without magnetometers or drugs, without any device, in fact, but an honest, reflective look at life. Many times we struggle to remember a name or to find a solution to a problem, then let the matter drop, and suddenly, in a moment of relaxation or unrelated thought, the answer appears in an impromptu flash of perception. Perception from where? From some subliminal source.

We all have innate faculties of perception which we rarely use or which we use instinctively. I have proof of this in a stunt I used to do following public lectures. When shaking hands with members of the audience, I often guessed or perceived their church affiliation. I would say to someone, "By the way, don't you happen to be a Presbyterian?" Or, to another, "Tell me, aren't you a Roman Catholic?" This divining of denominational traits was usually so accurate that I was accused of having engaged in planned research or espionage before the lecture period. Such was not the case. Most of the time I was as astonished at the accuracy fully as much as were my subjects.

One evening I said to a woman, "You must be either a Methodist or a Baptist." She replied with a gasp, "This is the most amazing thing I have ever heard! I was a Methodist all my life but I married a Baptist just two months ago!"

I call it perception, although it may merely be a natural development born of years of research and avid interest. Every successful salesman has it. Every parent knows what it is. Every artist in every field works with it as one of the tools of his trade.

Perhaps perception is nothing more than the sudden reward of a long spell of hard work. When photographer Edward Steichen won the prize at the International Exhibition in the Hague for his picture of Auguste Rodin, admirers said he had caught the sculptor's "inner spirit." They did not know that Steichen had studied and interviewed Rodin each Saturday for an entire year before he ever leveled the camera's eye at him. Even the phenomenal lighting on the photographic subject was, according to this master photographer, a matter of study and perceptivity. "Light," said Steichen, "is the magician."

What do you see when you look at a work of art or at a mountain or at a roving plane? Or, more important for our purpose, "What do you see when you look at life through your own innate power of perception?"

We are in control

For one thing, we see what we wish to see. It is possible to change every situation and condition in life by the simple act of perceiving that we can change our world by changing our thinking, our mental approach. This is something we can do instantly. Nobody can keep us from it. No one can interfere with our thinking. We have absolute control over our mind and its activity. No matter how many things seem wrong, we can correct them by perceiving that we can change our attitude toward them.

For another thing, we should recognize that everything in life, be it person or place, thoughts or things, carries within itself its own perceptive force, just as we do. We are not going to change another person. He must change himself. But first he must be true to his innate perception. Nature assures us of that. A flower perceives that it must seek the light as surely as a trout perceives that it must conquer rocks and rapids to reach its spawning pool, there to die. Perception is the ability to follow the process of release inherent in creation, and it is as basic as the truth that you and I must realize our deepest self by whatever path seems right and just for us.

Beyond the magnetometer and beyond peyote is the perception that the more earnestly we seek to see the commonly unseen, the more we find our deepest self. In life, as in art, the real and the true have a will to emerge. The authors of a book called *Eskimo* stated it pointedly when, in speaking of the Avilik Indian and his talent, they said, "As the carver holds the unworked ivory lightly in his hand, turning it this way and that, he whispers, 'Who are you? Who hides there?' And then he says, 'Ah, Seal!' He rarely sets out, at least consciously to carve, say, a seal, but picks up the ivory, examines it to find its hidden form and, if that is not immediately apparent, carves aimlessly until he sees it, humming or chanting as he works. Then he brings it out. Seal, hidden, emerges. It was always there. He did not create it, he released it. He helped it step forth."

There is always a center, a self, which has its own perception of what it can and will someday be.

"And if the doors of perception were cleansed," said William Blake, "everything would appear to be as it is, infinite."

So it would seem, for surely there are times when perception is the essence of insight, reflection, and awareness, and we know with certainty that things are not what they seem. Carried into the infinite field we perceive that what we call the commonplace may actually be a point of new revelation, what we frequently term sin is not really sin but an impulse on its way to goodness; failure is not failure, but an idea on its way to success; doubt is not doubt, but an experience on its way to faith; hate is no longer hate, it is love in embryo.

What do you see when you look at a rose or when, in the light of perception, you take another survey of the hidden mine of self?

PART TWO

THE COMMONLY UNHEARD

V ✱ INSPIRATION

On my study wall above the typewriter hangs a neatly printed sign: INSPIRATION IS THE ART OF BREATHING IN!

Many were the times I found help in this dictionary definition and equally many were the occasions when no inspiration came, hardly the impulse to breathe.

During one of these fallow periods on a blustery, blowing summer night I decided that what I needed was to take a trip. By all counts, I was inspirationless and the time had come for breathing in new sights, new scenes, new smells, and, most of all, new sounds. It was well and good for the monk to ask, "What do you hear when you listen to the wind?" but when all you hear is the blowing, it is time to break away.

One thing troubled me. I was always breaking away. My work and life at a state university were so structured that I was relatively free to come and go. In fact, a colleague whom I met on campus one day remarked, "I knew you were either here or somewhere else."

Suddenly it was this very freedom that annoyed me. What about people who could not take off and who found their inspiration without hying away to foreign ports and reporting newsreel-fashion what they saw and heard? The question haunted me, for my work *was* reporting and without something to report I was like a camera with nothing on which to click the shutter.

As I sat trying vainly to get an inspiration for a column which had reached its deadline, I asked myself, "What about those who must find strictly local, built-in sources of inspiration; professors tied to their jobs, businessmen chained to their offices, secretaries handcuffed to their desks, housewives shackled to the kitchen sink?" Throughout the academic year the campus was overrun by lecturers who came to share their exploits, travelogues, safaris, and their incredible journeys from Hunzaland to Zanzibar. What would these bold adventurers do if they, no less than I, were forced to stay at home and do their "breathing in" in the rarefied atmosphere of hometown?

The wind moaned and no inspiration came. Through the swaying shrubbery outside my study window I could see the light in our neighbor's kitchen in which the shadow of the busily occupied housewife flitted back and forth. She seemed inspired about something and yet, as far as I could judge, she was there in her home most of the 365 days, getting meals, serving meals, doing up the dishes only to start the cycle all over again the following morning, three times a day, a good thousand times a year.

Or what about the man on the other side of the lot, the bakery man who actually whistled while he worked? Every morning at five-thirty he warmed up his car and drove to work, there to start the ovens and the dough mixers and the cookie cutters and the bread slicers and all the rest. Year in and year out, the same doughnuts, Bismarcks, Napoleons, tarts, pies, cakes, and other patisserie emerged monotonously from the ovens in the same shapes, the same smells, the same taste with only slight seasonal deviations.

Across the street lived the banker with his hours regulated as methodically as the resounding strokes of the persistent clock atop St. Mary's Catholic Church. Every workaday morning at seven forty-five the banker left his house and walked to work to turn the same key in the same lock, to sit at the same desk, in the same chair, facing the same wall, and hearing the same sounds. What did he hear when he listened to the wind?

There was also the preacher whose study light burned almost in line with mine. His was a life completely at the beck and call of

842 parishioners who demanded a scintillating sermon every Sunday morning and some usuable thought to live by every Wednesday night. Rumor had it that the church was growing and that this young cleric had withstood the acid test of two years in a pastorate noted for its bickering. Evidently the preacher was vital, stimulating, and inspired. Yet the only traveling he ever engaged in was commuting to a seminary in Chicago, Illinois.

"Inspiration is the art of breathing in," said the maxim on my wall, and the wind blew on.

No need to travel

I knew a writer in British Columbia named Eric Nicol whose fresh and witty column in the Vancouver *Province* started the day silver bright for thousands of Canadians. He never let them down. He always had more to say than his quarter-page space allowed. The only trip he ever took was a slow boat to Japan, and he did not need to go there for subject matter; his inspirational sights were focused on the entire United Kingdom with many a telescopic side glance into the U.S.A. or wherever his fancy roamed.

Walter Lippmann is a case in point. Here is one of America's most brilliant interpreters, the "Great Elucidator," who rarely leaves 3525 Woodley Road, Washington, D.C. Yet his creative spirit ranges the world, assimilating and processing the thoughts and impressions of personalities whom he has never bothered to meet. Where did his voices come from?

Or consider August Derleth who was born within a block of my birthplace in Sauk City, Wisconsin. Author of some fifty books, anthologies of poetry and *belles lettres*, "Augie" was by modern standards practically a recluse. But he was far from running out of stock in his literary workshop. Evidently he just sat there and let the wind speak to him, always able to keep on "breathing in."

Once I visited an elderly Hutterian woman in a South Dakota commune. She was never wanting for sources of inspirational material. It surrounded her. Her children, her grandchildren, and a great-grandchild all lived within easy walking distance of her home. The unvarying daily routine of the colony constituted her life and her program for living, and she thrived on it though she had never been more than ten miles from her place of birth. Evidently her inspiration came from life easily within reach. The hymns sung at eventide, the commune sounds typical of the farm, the stories of the children, the exchange of reminiscences, the change of seasons, these provided all she needed to light the interest of her life.

When I stopped to call on her one day I regaled her with accounts of my traveling, feeling that by so doing I would transport her to far-away places and permit her to escape from the colony acres for a while. She listened patiently as she sat near the window with her knitting, rocking and knitting while I talked. When I finished she nodded understandingly and, without pausing in her rocking, said, "You have been to all those places and I have been nowhere, and here we are in the same place at the same time."

Against the raging wind I argued that travel is a legitimate and effective remedy for inspirational deficiency and it is pleasant to take, especially in small doses. But at the moment I wondered whether it was possibly making a hypochondriac out of me.

Ideas knocking at the door

On the desk before me lay a neat sheaf of yellow pages and six #2 Ticonderoga pencils, my prerequisites for any sort of writing spree. As I looked at them I remembered a nephew of mine whose first book had been chosen by a major book club after he had struggled long and hard for a breakthrough in inspiration.

"I was trying and trying to write," he said, "but nothing came through and nothing seemed to jell when suddenly there was a rap at the door. I called out, 'Come in!' but no one came. The knocking continued. I opened the door and there was no one in sight. 'That's strange,' I thought, and went back to try to write. The knocking came again. I jumped up and opened the door and shouted, 'Who are you? Where are you?' Then something said to me, 'Here we are. We are your ideas. We have been trying to get in but you won't give us a chance.' There they were: ideas suddenly crowding in on me, gathering around me, sitting in my lap, talking to me like mad!"

It had sounded like an interesting fantasy when he told it, but now with the windows rattling and the shutters clanking and with no knocking at *my* study door, it was not so impressive. I heard no raps. All I caught sound of was the time sentinel atop St. Mary's tolling out eight pedantic strokes in the wind outside my window.

Inspiration. Where would I find it?

I got up to sharpen the Ticonderogas, which were already needle sharp, and as I did so, I noticed the university newspaper lying open to the calendar of events for this particular night and announcing a campus lecture in which a student of mine was reviewing Wolfgang Kohler's book, *The Mentality of Apes.*

It occurred to me as I turned the crank on the pencil sharpener that a chimpanzee could have done this just as well as I, and that a spider monkey might have jotted down more ideas on the yellow sheets than I had done in the past two hours. Who, I wondered, would go to a lecture on a blustery night like this? Only an ape.

But I remembered lectures I had given on stormy nights and recalled how grateful I had been whenever the door opened and another listener slipped in. I remembered those who made a special effort to drop around and how agonizing it was to talk to empty seats . . . and how a teacher should by rights keep in touch with the work of his students. . . . The next thing I knew I had placed the six pencils neatly on the unused yellow sheets and found myself in the out-of-doors with my head against the wind.

Nueva, the chimpanzee

Interestingly enough a good crowd was on hand for the lecture. Others must have felt as I did about coming out, or perhaps we were simply complimenting ourselves on our place on the evolutionary ladder. At any rate the meeting had an informality refreshingly different from sessions usually held here in staid old "Senate Chamber." I was glad I had come. Even the wind had a different sound. It provided, as the student-lecturer suggested, the jungle background through which we might catch the telltale echoes of our earlier environment.

Soon I was hearing other sounds. I was hearing about Nueva.

Nueva was the lady chimpanzee who played the leading role in an experiment in creative thinking. She was the protagonist in Kohler's book, and tonight she was brought to life by a young man who was out to sell himself as a public speaker. In descriptive style he made us visualize Nueva's imprisonment. Through careful word painting we were shown Madame Chimp confined to an eight-foot-square cage, moodily gazing out through her bars at freedom's world. We were cajoled into seeing her watery eyes peering into space as if seeking to fathom the mystery of her place in the eternal scheme of things, listening as if to catch some sound, some hint as to how and why she should adjust herself to her imprisonment.

We were assured that Nueva was hungry. We were persuaded that she was a stranger. We were made to feel her loneliness with such intensity that our own sense of loneliness increased.

"She is saying to herself," our speaker advised, "'Do the bars confine me or protect me?' She is asking, 'Where did I come from? Why am I here? Where am I going?' And all she hears is the wailing of the wind!"

Dramatically the student described how Nueva's captor—"a mysterious personage, like a god he must have seemed to the chimpanzee"—entered the scene and placed a luscious banana tantalizingly near Nueva outside her cage, laid it close, but not close enough for Nueva to reach it. Close, but out of reach. Close, but not within her grasp. Close, but just beyond her touch. There it lay and Nueva gazed at it long and longingly. Then she stretched out her hairy arm and flexed her spiny fingers, all in vain. Hopefully she tried to squeeze her trembling body through the unyielding bars and agonizingly stretched out her hand again, only to find the banana still beyond her reach. Frightened she drew back, gasping for breath.

Squatting frustrated in her cage, she once more listened for a sound, a whisper, a voice. She closed her eyes, as if by shutting out reality, reality might become more clear, as if by admitting her limitations she might be rewarded with a sense of knowing beyond her own. Suddenly she flung open her eyes and stared around, as if she *had* heard something, as if an inner voice *had* spoken. And then Nueva wept. In a voice that was a murmur of lamentation, she shook her head hopelessly and wept.

Now there had been placed in the cage ever since Nueva's drama began a stick sufficient in length to provide the extension Nueva needed to reach the coveted banana. The stick had been lying there throughout her agonizing ordeal. Would she recognize that this had a bearing on her problem? Would she be able to fit together the intricate creative process that the stick, properly used, would extend her reach? Was there an intelligence somewhere that would counsel her? Had she ever seen any other chimp in a similar situation confronted by a similar circumstance? Had she anyone to guide her, or was she truly alone, isolated, a stranger in an even stranger universe? Hopefully she fixed her eyes on her captor, who stood outside the cage, statuesque and unyielding. Not a sign, not a nod, not a blink of the eye came from him. Nueva looked and listened until it seemed as if the silence would have to break, but there came no whisper and no sound, except the fateful moaning of the wind.

After a dramatic pause, our student turned the pages of Kohler's book. "Nueva," he read in actorial tones, "flings herself on the ground on her back in a gesture most eloquent of despair . . . between lamentations and entreaties time passes, until about seven minutes after the fruit has been exhibited to her, she suddenly casts a look at the stick! Ceasing her moaning, she seizes the stick, stretches it out of the cage, and succeeds, though somewhat clumsily, in drawing the banana within her reach!"

Having read these words, the speaker placed both hands melodramatically on the pages of the book and stood with head raised as if he himself sought to importune the Keeper of his cage with some silent, solemn invocation. Putting the question primarily to himself, he asked, "From where did the answer come? How did the impulse get through from sender to receiver? Through what unseen transmitter did it travel? With whom did it originate? *Who told Nueva to reach down and grasp this wand of inspiration?*"

No one laughed. No one stirred. And no one answered. Even the "wand of inspiration" did not seem just then too archaic a phrase for modern use. "All we know," the student was saying, "is that the keeper of the cage left the stick lying conveniently within easy reach and there were no strings attached."

Everyone smiled good-naturedly at that.

All I could think of just then was a row of sharpened pencils lying on a stack of yellow pages in the low-burning light of my study. All I could hear were the voices in the wind telling me that if we do not find within our reach the "wand of inspiration" wherever we are, we will never find it no matter where we go. Suddenly I felt myself involuntarily breathing in, half-saying to myself, "Cease your moaning! Seize the stick! Stretch it out of the cage and draw the elusive object of your affection within your reach. No one is ever left without a wand of inspiration!"

When I returned home I wrote the student a letter, and it was amazing how reciprocal everything suddenly became. Write a letter and you are traveling. Compliment someone and you are complimenting yourself. Help another person in his quest and you receive guidelines for your own seeking. Give a friend an idea and you are rewarded with ideas in return. Even a chimp, demonstrating originality in using a stick, inspired a man to write a book.

Seldom will a professor admit that he learns as much from his students as they learn from him, and I am not saying that I made such a confession in my note of appreciation, but it was significant that as soon as I had written the letter, inspiration was knocking at my door and voices whispering in the wind began enumerating some of the magic wands of inspiration within my easy reach.

What were these wands?

The plain sense of need was one of them, need to satisfy the hunger of the body or the soul. Had it not always been so? Need for survival inspired man to mobilize his resources; need for solution to problems inspired ingenuity; need for wisdom, study; need for answers, research; need for faith, the practice of prayer; need for a cause, inspired commitment.

The stimulation of need and of love

In all directions of life *need* confronts us. To reach a goal, to grasp an idea, to lay hold of a dream, to hear some voice of guidance, even to reach a banana outside the cage, *need* stimulates and mobilizes inspiration if we are willing so to approach the awareness of our need. In fact, need takes on a different meaning if we see it as a challenge to our creativity.

And love was surely a wand, a wand born of need, born of a need for love.

Perhaps this was the housewife's secret, love for those who in turn fulfilled her need for love.

It could be that the baker's inspiration was love, too, and through it fullfillment of the need and love of work.

And the banker's inspiration may have been love, and through it love of finance or money or service; and the preacher's wand could easily have been love for someone or for the many and through it love for the Lord, or, perhaps, he would have put it the other way around.

Love, no doubt, extends one's reach and is always reciprocal. Love for life inspires health, and love for health, life; love for beauty, art, and love for art, beauty; love for harmony, music; love for achievement, labor; for expression, creativity; for adventure, courage; for mercy, sacrifice; love for others, selflessness—the list was endless. But always it was love, fulfilling a need, as the stick fulfilled a need for Nueva.

That nephew of mine who imagined he had heard ideas knocking at his door had a love for flying. His wands of inspiration were the airlanes, and for some six years he had piloted jets in America and abroad. One day, just for the thrill of it, he flew an open cockpit plane.

"For the first time in flying," he said, "I heard the wind. . . ."

As Anne Morrow Lindbergh, in her day, captured the mood of sea and sky in her *Listen! The Wind!* so he caught the music of the wind and the elements as he sat open to the sky.

"The wind has many voices," said rancher Raymond Carlson. "There is the wind in the pine tops when you are spending a few weeks in the mountains. There is the song of the wind caressing the waves of the ocean when you are vacationing by the sea. But nothing is as musical and soothing as the wind when you are trying to make a living out of a few hundred head of cattle on a small spread in the dry and arid land, and you hear the whirling blades of the windmill, attuned to the whimsy of the wind, assuring you that there will be water and that thirsty cattle will drink."

And now *I* heard the wind, not in any far-off place or roaring plane, but in my study late at night, and the wind was saying that inspiration has no special cosmic center, but that it is found wherever we *will* to find it. It was saying that a dramatist can discover it in the rise and fall of empires or on a quiet street of hometown. A musician can hear it in a storm or in the silence of a moonlight night. A writer, willing to listen, can recognize it in war or peace. A prophet finds it in the exodus of his people or in the murmur of a newborn child.

I had to conclude that inspiration is a matter of discernment, as much as it is love and need. Discernment of suffering inspires charity; discernment of pride, anonymity; of talent, investment; of crisis, wisdom; of service, appreciation; discernment of nature, kinship.

The cause that inspires

I recalled another windy, blustery night when, on a West Coast campus, the college community was stirred to fever pitch because a young man convicted of murder was to be executed by the state on the following morning. A group of students, violently opposed to capital punishment, held a meeting and delivered their impassioned pleas. There was no question about the man's guilt, no argument about the atrocity of the crime, but the students had their cause, and I was pleading it with them: a revolt against the concept of the state's taking a life for a life. That night, when campus and people were divided and blown about in the storm of hatred and revenge, I went to my office and wrote until morning, pouring out on paper what I hoped would be a big voice in the cause of humanity and understanding. Nothing ever came of it excepting the remembrance, now, of the fire of inspiration and the howling wind.

Freedom marchers, conscientious objectors, campus advocates of "the right to be heard," leftists, rightists, super-patriots, reactionaries, religious zealots, it is the cause that stirs them, it is the cause that inspires, and whether we agree with them or not, we learn that if, as we grow older, we lose the spirit of inspiration instead of investing it in thoughtful approach to solving problems, we have closed our hearts to the voices in the wind.

The lexographers were quite right when, in looking for a word to describe the essence of creativity, they hit upon *inspiration,* a definition of the *breath of life,* as if to say that when we cease being inspired we cease to live, and as if to insinuate that it is up to us how long and how richly we wish both to live and to create.

Evidently both living and creating are commandments of the heart and fulfill themselves as perfectly in little things as in things that seem great. Wherever we are, we are never left without our "wands of inspiration" whether in an upstairs study on a stormy night or in a chimpanzee's cage within the pages of a book.

I had an idea. Why not write my column on "Inspiration" and title it, "*What do you hear when you listen to the wind?*"

And why not begin by saying, "Inspiration is the art of breathing in!"

VI * RECOGNITION

The first sound we heard in the morning was the drone of a chain saw. Nothing else. No song of a bird, no wind, no waves against the beach. The morning was hushed and breathless as if listening with us to the incessant whir of the saw that was like a wounded animal trying to hide its groans. But the longer it cried, the more it seemed to be boasting about its pain, until it haunted us with the sense of its struggle.

Who else in the Kootenay Valley was listening, I wondered? Who else was saying, "They're clearing the right of way for the power line?" Who else, besides my wife and me, looked anxiously to the hills?

Suddenly the power saw screamed in a high pitch of victory against which there was an explosive, cracking sound, and a man's echoing cry, "Timber! Let 'er roll!"

A tree swayed in its place against the sky and fell with a voice almost human. Its years—fifty, a hundred, two hundred—fell with it. All it represented to itself and to the world fell with it and perished. Its outstretched limbs cushioned it gently after the killing stroke. It settled slowly, quivered, and lay down to die while its branches stretched out over the earth like a prophet whipped and stoned until he felt no pain.

The man with the power saw wiped his forehead with his sleeve and proceeded to the next tree only an arm's length away. The blue wisp of smoke from the saw rolled upward, the whirring teeth bit into the brown bark and the droning sound with its make-believe agony began again.

The week before, Lorena and I had been in Haiti at a voodoo service. The scenes and sounds of the falling trees took us back to the enchanted scene. The man with the smoking power saw was the *houngan,* the voodoo priest. He wove the spell. The slashers in their red helmets, cigarettes clamped in their lips, swinging their axes as they chopped the branches from the fallen monarch, they were the *hounsi,* the voodoo acolytes, invoking the spirits. The animals that ran frightened from the brush, the birds that flew away scared, they were the *loa,* the discarnate entities. We were the credulous worshipers, praying for we knew not what unless it was for the hope of finding meaning in the commonly unheard—the death cry of a tree.

The need to forget

But who wants to live at this late date without electric power straight off a high line, no matter how remote his mountain hide-away may be?

Next year we would already be saying, "How did we ever get along with the old lighting system?"

The year after that one of us would probably ask, "Were there three of those big pines up there where the transformer stands?"

To which the other would answer, "I thought there were four. How quickly one forgets."

Metaphysicians put great stress on the need for forgetting, which they call the science of oblivescence. They contend that thought and existence are indivisible and that if we change our thinking we change our life as surely as a shift in the wind changes the direction of the weather vane.

What a patient needs to do, they say, is practice oblivescence, for if he can erase from his deepest level of consciousness unpleasant thoughts and remembrances, he will be well. If he asks, "How can I get the strength to do this?" you must tell him that it is not a question of getting it from anywhere but of using it, for he already has it. It is like seeing an obstruction in the road and asking, "Where are my arms to help me remove it?" Recognition is the art of knowing that you already have what you need and that the questions you ask are already answered though the voice that speaks within you is commonly unheard.

If you are willing to listen you will hear the voice and it will tell you that the cause and the reason of things become clear if you project yourself into the future, recognizing *now* that all things will work together for good *later*. The presupposition being, of course, that you live up to your highest and best, and the requirement being that you proceed on faith; neither of which is simple or easy, and both of which consistently refute cold logic and rational thought. You must recognize that God is revealed but not found in the universe, just as the mind is revealed but not found in the brain, or as love is revealed but not found in any examination of the human heart.

It is not easy to answer the question, "What do you hear in the fall of a tree?" It requires, as has been said, tremendous courage and faith to be philosophical when something meaningful and loved in your life falls with a cry and leaves an open space against your perspective of the totality of things. It is equally difficult to project oneself into the future while haunted by remembrances of how things might have been—difficult to see the light before the lights come on or to recognize that something may be worth the price when the price seems unseemly high.

Before we ever staked out the ground for our cabin it was necessary to get a workman with a bulldozer to level out the hillside. He sat in his giant machine on an overhang above the lane and yelled to me below, "We're coming down!"

I called back, "Don't come down there! You're in direct line with the silver spruce!"

"I'll miss that!" he shouted.

The screeching chains of the "Cat" began to roll like the *Wehrmacht* of old. Blue vapor belching from the upright exhaust, levers clanking against an orchestral frenzy of spitting rocks and dust, the scraping hooves of the behemoth thundered down. The muscular operator tried frantically to bring it under control. Defiantly it outmaneuvered him and plunged like a cart of death into and over the twenty-foot-high silver spruce, pulverizing it into a mangled refuse of sticks and dust.

The workman was casually apologetic. With an oath, he thanked God that the spruce had been there or he'd have gone straight into the lake. With a grin he said, "It's only a tree and I can get you another."

I walked away, half-ashamed that I could cry about a tree and half-concerned that I would just as soon have seen the driver and the "Cat" plunge headlong into the water and get out as best they could.

How does one hear the voice that says, "In time there will be other trees"? Or, "Someday you will look back on this and it will all seem just another part of life"? Is it humanly possible to console oneself at the time of a distressing happening with the assurance that, "This, too, shall pass away"? The question is, how could I have heard, at that moment, the hillside as it sings now with trees tall and growing and as beautiful as the spruce once stood? Where does one get the vision or the courage to recognize that the spirit of that which *was* makes more sacred and beautiful that which is to be?

Hearing the voice within

Evidently recognition of this kind requires a great deal of faith, blind faith, and a great deal of awareness of a voice within, for surely there is this kind of whispering if we but take time to listen. We are never left alone in any situation or under any circumstance.

Again and again in my research I find those who are convinced that they recognize an inner guidance as if it were a voice speaking to them. Some say it is God calling, and I know that psychiatrists will tell you that the line between inspirations of this kind and aberrations of another kind is a very fine line and that the distance separating a saint from a psychopath or a prophet from a paranoiac is narrower than a razor's edge.

It is just as well that some of the great minds and some of the great men who shaped our lives were never psychoanalyzed.

Consider, for example, the Athenian teacher standing before the tribunal which had sentenced him to death for misguiding the youth of his time. "O my judges," he said, "a most wonderful thing has happened to me! You see, I have a voice within, a benign being whom I call my daemon. Always in times past he has stopped me if I were about to act in some way not right. But now that this fate has come upon me, this sentence of death, this which a man might consider the worst of ills, neither when I left home this morning nor when I came up to this judgment hall did my voice speak to me. It did not stop me as if my coming here were ill. What is the reason? I will tell you. I think that what has happened to me must be a *good* thing; and we must have been mistaken when we supposed that death was an evil. I have strong proof for this, for otherwise my daemon would have stopped me and told me otherwise."

There were judges in the tribunal who looked at each other and then looked back at Socrates and touched a finger to their head and murmured, "This is what happens to men when they become too philosophical"—"Whom the gods would destroy they first make mad"—"The first sign of insanity is to hear voices." But there were some who walked home thoughtfully that day, hearing within themselves voices of their own arguing pro and con about man's capacity for understanding, and man's destiny in the kind of a complicated world in which he lives, and who wished with all their hearts that they had the courage and the faith to look at life—and death—as did this unhandsome but gifted teacher of the people.

For what a lonely life it is if we live it alone, without the voice within. What a desolate existence if, as Socrates himself suggested, we never pause to examine the deeper reaches of our lives.

There was the Nazarene, a man who went about doing good and loving mercy, and those who were acquainted with Him felt it not unreasonable that He should have been guided by some inner recognition of what He chose to call His Father's voice. To those who knew Him it was no fairy tale when it was rumored that a heavenly chorus had heralded His birth, that a voice out of the sky had spoken at His baptism, and that, after His death, an angel appeared to those who sought His body and greeted them by saying, "Why seek ye the living among the dead?"

Many there were and many there are today who believe not a word of this and who contend that legends are merely the secret weapons of deception. Many there are who insist that there is a type of person who needs something to worship and someone to deify, and that there will always be those who are happy to supply fulfillment for this need. But others, having felt within themselves something suggestive of a consciousness similar to that of the Nazarene, having heard the faint whisper of what might have been the voice of the "Father," and having caught for a brief moment their own concept of a heavenly vision—these pursue the quest quietly on their own or, perhaps, in fellowship with Him.

There was Mahatma Gandhi, the liberator of his people, and because of the nature of his life those who followed him were not dismayed when he said, "My authority is the voice." He meant the voice of all the prophets and of all the faiths, but he also meant a spirit voice that guided and directed the strategy of his cause, a voice that melted differences into unity as far as his goals were concerned, a voice that said through him, "Our battle will be won not by the number of enemies we can kill, but by the number of enemies in whom we can kill the desire to kill."

When, at a meeting designed for peace and prayer, an assassin fired three bullets into his defenseless body, the Mahatma said, "Do the poor man no harm." It was a voice speaking through him.

I met those in India who said that Gandhi was a fanatic, given to visions and to too much *soma*, but across the length and breadth of the subcontinent that was his home, his spirit lives and speaks through the millions who recognize that a prophet walked among them in their time.

So it seemed to me when I reflected on the chain saw and the trees that came toppling down. So it was when I thought of the bulldozer that bedeviled the silver spruce. I turn on the lights and the electric power in the cabin and I look out at the hillside and at the trees that are growing . . . and all the world becomes as much a riddle as it does an answer to my groping.

Learning from silence

Something says to me: if you listen too anxiously or try to figure things out on a scale that suits your mind, you cannot hear the voice, and if you beg and plead for perfect understanding you will be annoyed by the silence. But if you are content with the presence of the divine quiet, you will get your message and if you will keep on with your work and your life you will surely hear the whisper of God.

Recognition!

Emerson, whose phrases are much too pretty unless you draw your chair up close to nature, said, "Over everything stands its daemon or its soul, and, as the form of a thing is reflected by the eye, so the soul of a thing is reflected by a melody. The sea, the mountain, Niagara, and every flower-bed, pre-exists or super-exists in precantations, which sail like odors in the air, and when any man passes by with an ear sufficiently fine he overhears them and endeavors to write down the notes without diluting or depraving them."

We may not understand the full import of this Emersonian dictum. It may have been written, as indeed it was, for poets and musicians, but for the moment it makes us feel that someone has interpreted a point of life for us better than we could have done it for ourselves.

To say that we recognize an affinity with "the sea, the mountain," and so on and that sometimes we overhear their voices—as I felt I overheard the death cry of a tree—this could be a dark and dangerous saying if we said it too loudly in the presence of our logical, positivistic friends. It is like asking, "What do you hear when you listen to the wind?" But I cannot escape, nor can most of us, from the authority of these words. They mean something and they mean more as life becomes more meaningful.

After the silver spruce came down, I sat in the early evening and watched the sun lower itself behind the mountains with its customary determined quiet. I realized again that there is a world —the cosmic world—about which I knew so little that my knowledge of it had no influence on it one way or another. It was a world independent of me and of what I thought or wished, as independent as the bulldozer was in its rushing down upon the tree.

I had not a ghost of a chance of holding back the sun or of hurrying its reappearing or of influencing it in its course. It was completely and totally transcendent. Yet, often in its afterglow, I caught a fleeting hint that whatever governed it governed me, and something assured me beyond a doubt that despite the fall of trees or men or the coming or going of prophets or philosophers, all is well and everything is in most excellent hands. I did not know what all this meant unless it was my monitor's way of giving me a recognition of truth beyond the common manifestation. Occasionally something does speak to us from within as if to remind us of the truth and faith upon which we must rest our case for life. A proverb has it that nature gives us new speech and silence teaches us new understanding, to which I add that one moment of such inspiration more than prepares us for another week of work.

My work at the cabin is usually a matter of meeting deadlines and whatever inspiration comes to me often comes late at night. I can usually recognize when it comes, but not how or why. There is generally no use trying to write in the early morning because nothing comes through, or I look out of the windows and see that the hillside needs mowing or the workshop needs cleaning or the boat or the beach or the yard requires attention. I never have any trouble finding a trouble spot when the day is just beginning. The night is different.

When the crimson afterglow changes to the heliotrope mystique so typical of the Kootenay and the first star appears above the Selkirks, that is when I feel that I or anyone can be a ready channel for creative thought. A faint, nearly soundless stirring of the breeze keeps the lake restless with a rhythmic, throbbing pulse, the water is a shimmering mirror reflecting reddish-blue clouds through a skiff of evening mist. Unconsciously you hear the soft, playful splashing of the kokanee trout as if they want to call your attention to their world; as if they were saying, "Do not think that because this lake is only four miles wide and a hundred miles long we do not belong to the oceans and the seas. We are here at this particular time and place, but we are also part of the everlasting time-and-tide that governs and directs all waters. Life here is life everywhere."

And the strange part about all of this is that though you are alone in a mountain cabin you are nearer to more worlds than you are when in a city with all its sights and sounds. At least, you can identify yourself with more worlds and with more people because you get a feeling that everyone, no matter who or what he is or where or how he is faring, would be grateful for a touch of quiet, if for no other reason than that he would interpret sounds in a new way when he returned to his noisy world.

Sometimes there are oppressive nights, too, and on one of these I was holed in for a long session with pencils sharpened and plenty of yellow paper and my Schnauzer dog dozing on the sofa behind me. I had a story to do on Chichicastenango, the fabulous Guatemalan "ghost village" that springs to life on market days and fills the air with incense and the chanted prayers of censor-swinging Mayan priests. It was exciting, magical material, as rare as this night was rare for Kootenay. An enervating night, as I have said, hot and sticky with moths and beetles tapping at the windows and buzzing at the screen door close to where I sat.

A *night's lesson*

But for some reason it was an exceptionally good night for writing, and I felt I was doing well until, after several hours, the roar of a car on the mountainous highway brought me to a serious point of concern. Lorena had taken some friends to Spokane earlier that day to catch a plane and she had half-promised to be back at nine or nine-thirty. It was ten-thirty when I looked at my watch and I found it difficult after that to keep my mind on the job at hand. Out of the swelter of the night and into my mind came a sudden, distressing thought, "What if something has happened to her?"

I immediately tried to dismiss the thought, believing, as I do, that we bring into reality these purely subjective fantasies through recognition. The thing to do is to deny them! And I proceeded to do so. Through various techniques and what I considered to be proven processes, I put from my mind any thought of accident, tragedy, or mishap of any kind. Lorena, I told myself, is a good driver, has driven in many parts of the world, has crossed the country alone, and knows the Kootenay roads as well as anyone.

Eleven o'clock. Eleven-twenty. Another lone car zoomed along the highway above the lane, its sound funneling out into a silence deeper than any I had ever heard in all my many nights at the cabin. The moths and scarabs tapped at the windows and scratched at the screen, and it seemed impossible to me that I had never noticed them or given them a thought until this night. Were they something new, something ominous, a sign of some sort? Deny them!

Eleven-thirty, and I could no longer keep my mind on Chichicastenango or on old St. Thomas Church or on Maya-Quiche priests performing their hypnotic rituals in the Guatemalan hills.

Then, in a split-second moment when I was denying and affirming that nothing had happened, that nothing could happen—when I was half-persuaded that something *had* happened or I would never have had the premonition in the first place—when it was almost as though I heard a voice—I heard a car on the highway, heard the car, the screech of brakes, the piercing bark of the Schnauzer as he leaped out of his sleep and sprang against the screen barking frantically, and in that instant I swooped him up as if to keep him from affirming what I refused to accept—and as I stood there holding him under my arm hardly daring to move, I heard a man's voice on the highway cry out, "She's dead!"

In that moment when time stood still there passed through my mind everything that Lorena and I had ever meant to each other, everything that I had done and left undone, everything that I had said and left unsaid, and already I wondered why with all my appreciation, I had never appreciated our relationship enough. All this was spun off the reel of mind in less time than it took me to put down the dog, grab a flashlight, throw open the door, and start running up the lane. Behind me, barking furiously and pawing at the screen was the Schnauzer. Above me on the lane, a sudden sound, the roar of a car engine, a screaming take-off, and car lights streaming away around the mountainous road.

How strange and unreal this was. How still and haunted the night, how suddenly one's world changes, how subtle the recognition, the precognition, the voices of life! Then I was on the highway and where the black-top road meets the lane my light flared on the glistening brown and white body of a deer, struck down by a car.

I stood there, I don't know how long, stood there lost in thought in a way never quite experienced before. It was not the question about God, not even an inquiry into the meaning and purpose of things—those were beyond me anyway. I stood there thinking about the question of *me*. And just now that was beyond me, too.

Deer are often killed on the Kootenay highway, but this one—this one was different. Who runs into a deer with his car and says, "*She's* dead!" instead of "It's dead!" or "He's dead!"? Who *times* these happenings? What is the lesson that the killers of the deer had to learn? What was *my* lesson? Or was mine already learned when I discovered it was a deer that had been sacrificed?

I dragged the warm, broken body into the deep grass and walked with my questions back to the cabin to press the trembling dog in my arms.

Lorena came almost immediately, honking the horn in a customary signal that all was well.

"I hope you weren't worried," she said.

"Why should I be worried?" I said. "You're a good driver."

"The fog was so thick," she explained. "I had to crawl along. You know how it is on that stretch before you get to the border. And it didn't lift until just the last few miles. I could stand a drink."

"So could I," I said, "if you can stand a story."

From the patio at midnight you can see whatever you are looking for: mystery or miracle. You can hear whatever voices you may have in mind. You can sit there and reflect—reflect on the sound of a power saw, if you wish, or on a falling tree, or even on bugs and beetles tapping on the screen.

You might even reflect on a deer caught in a moment of inexplicable destiny or on Maya-Quiche priests swinging their censors in Guatemalan hills.

The love of life, as a wise man once said, at any and every level of experience is a religious impulse. To recognize this may be the beginning of wisdom and a reasonable approach to an understanding of the voice within.

VII * INTUITION

Among the men who changed my way of thinking was a shoemaker in Görlitz, Germany. I have a feeling that I must have lived in his time, say around 1600. Wandering into his shop under the pretense of having him examine a rundown heel, let us say, I probably hung around to hear him speak, not about shoes, but about life.

I must have met him when both he and I were in our mid-twenties, a time of deep and earnest questing. Though we were of the same age, he had already found what I was looking for; the secret of innate knowledge or what is classically called intuitionalism. I have learned since then that intuition has many meanings. Popularly it means playing your hunches. Philosophically it is direct apprehension of truth. Physiologically it is synonymous with instinct. Religiously it is divine insight. Metaphysically it is enlightenment.

Whatever it was or is, I longed to possess it. In fact, as I have said, that must have been why I kept going back to the shoemaker's shop on the quaint and shady street across from Görlitz Square, not far from the Church of St. Peter and Paul. The shoemaker had this instant knowledge. If, as we now know from our contemporary records, that a bat was the sudden inspiration for the discovery of radar, and that the common sea nettle furnished the design for parachutes, why should not a maker of shoes be a legitimate guide for discovering the secret of intuition?

In romance I remember when I first passed his window and saw him sitting at his cobbler's bench. Around him on the floor and on the two sturdy oak shelves near the polishing wheel were boots and shoes and sandals and a row of lasts in cubbyholes like wine bottles lying in their stalls. And in his teeth, that first time I saw him, was a rose; actually a rosebud, deep yellow. Most cobblers, I suppose, have their mouths full of nails ready for work. He had the stem of the rose casually between his lips without affectation or pretense.

The man's serenity filled me with envy and delight. He was of medium height, gray-eyed, with a short, thin beard and a thick crop of black hair rather long in the back and covered on top with a brown *mütze* that matched his lengthy leather apron. When I ventured up the two wooden steps and pushed open the weathered door, a bell tinkled above my head. It was a happy, friendly sound and soon I stood before the man, twisting my foot so that he could see what my step was doing to my footgear. He asked me to remove my shoe and said he would repair it at once, suggesting with a sigh that no one should go through life obliquely.

His voice was feeble and strangely old for so young a man, but it reflected the unassuming and sensitive quality of one who apparently asked nothing of life but the chance to explore his reason for being in the world and, above all, hinted at his supposition that since he *was* in it he had a right to know how and where instant knowledge could be attained.

I felt that he would have been just as unpretentious had he been the Burgermeister of Görlitz or the pastor primarius or the village doctor in this ancient town of 20,000 souls. He would have been just as content had he been a peasant farmer or a liveryman or a forest dweller in the thick acres of timber that enclosed the village. He was a shoemaker, had been one since he was thirteen because his peasant parents were poor and he had to work. He was by all odds the master shoemaker's most valued apprentice.

Awakening to one's own potential

Is that what intuition does for a person, I wondered? Does it take you aside and say, "Now, see here, you are *you*. There is no need wishing you were someone else, because you aren't. There is no possible point in saying you would be happier if you were taller or shorter or if you had grown up in a family with money or with brains or with social connections, or that you wished you had grown up with no family at all. Unless wishing causes you to improve yourself or change your lot in life, stop wishing and start working."

Intuition, I had no doubt, was, to begin with, some such counselor, a monitor awaking oneself to one's potential, one's uniqueness, one's special assignment in his particular period in time and space. But because I was sure it was also instant knowledge, back to the shoemaker I went, always unable, however, to come right out and say, "I hear you are a most wonderful intuitionalist. How did you get this way and how can I get this way?"

My spying on him told me that almost every evening when his working day was done, he would sit near his lighted tallow lamp in his side-street home after his chores were over, and he would read and write or visit with friends. Surely this was normal enough in an unmarried man. Sundays he would go to church to find out, as he once said off-handedly to me, what he could about the revelation of God in theology. In the afternoon he would walk the Sabbath countryside to discover God in nature. Occasionally when someone told him that there was a strange feeling of a "presence" about him, he simply smiled and said in his quiet way, "Isn't this true of everyone?"

I thought about this a great deal whenever I walked the streets of Görlitz and asked myself whether this might be the heart and core of intuition, the realization that we have a "presence," that everyone has a "presence," and that this is a way of trying to understand the depth and dimensions we instinctively sense at times but do not comprehend. Is it possible that if we realized we project a "presence" we would never feel frustrated or depressed? Surely we would never feel lonely or alone, if we realized that. So often when I did my best, I felt it was not really my deepest or my most realizable best. Now I wondered whether this might have been intuition's way of telling me that I would do better next time or, perhaps, the "presence" had actually accomplished what I felt had been left undone. But only an intuitionalist like the shoemaker would have had the insight and the grace to acknowledge the "presence" in others or to simply say, "Is not this true of everyone?"

To be frank, I admired him as much for his talents as for his character. In the first place, he made excellent shoes and took pride in his meticulous work without actually *being* proud. Secondly, he was a linguist, speaking eight or more languages as easily as I spoke one. Third, he was never interested in little things—the village gossip, the squabbles of the city fathers, or the destruction of the Spanish armada—all these, he figured, would pass.

Man's fragmented vision

Important to him was the subject: how do we as individuals come to an understanding of our relationship with the Power that made us and sustains us, and yet which seems to hide itself from us? This he answered in a most wonderful way by explaining that what God comprehends as ONE is, to our limited apprehension, TWO. Because of our finite nature we always see things only in part, in fragments, as it were, and never as God sees them. "The darkness and the light are both alike to Thee, O God," but to us they seem to be two conditions, two circumstances. And so it is with life, we are unable to see ourselves as ONE.

So the shoemaker said, "In what man holds to be right or true, there is always an element present in God's comprehension of it, which man fails to integrate. Both man's right and wrong are imperfect to God, for God's right is man's right AND wrong synthesized. Man is limited and he cannot see the whole of God's ONE. There is always an aspect of things which he sees and does not see. His is surface sight. It is as if he looked at the surface of the ocean and tried to fathom what is in its depths. The more we try to see things as God sees them, the more their basic unity is revealed."

I was never quite the same after hearing this and when I say that the shoemaker changed my thinking, this was part of it. I used to have a habit of judging and appraising people by seeing them as black or white as far as their characters were concerned, but now I knew that there was a part of their nature I could not see; no one could see it or know it but God. The guilty man, the condemned man, the malcontent, the misanthrope, and the like—I saw them only with surface vision.

The same was true of those I accounted as good men, great men. There was a morality I could see and a morality I could not see. God saw the whole man, and the more I kept this fact in mind, the more understanding I became of all men. Could this be part of intuition's mission? At any rate, this the shoemaker taught me, and again I asked, "Where does he get knowledge of this kind?"

Obviously he got it *intuitively* and not by study merely or by cobbling or by chewing at the stem of a rose. But obdurate villagers of Görlitz simply shrugged off any such conjecture and said, "He has one of those strange retentive minds that remembers everything it reads. There is no mystery about him."

If this were true, why would not every good scholar or student or retentive reader be an intuitionalist? They weren't. Book knowledge they had, to be sure, and logical reasoning and a deep appraisal of current data, but if it were only information and facts that were passed from generation to generation, how would the world ever progress? There were definitely individuals who by an intuitional leap discovered new countries of thought, new empires of belief, and opened doors to new kingdoms of experiences which laughed at logic and ridiculed the claims of reason.

I was never willing to accept the rational explanation for this neighborly shoemaker being what he was simply because "he has one of those strange retentive minds." And I suppose the main reason for my refusal to accept it was because of my secret hope that somewhere in each of us is a mysteriously hidden switch-of-the-spirit which by a subtle touch admits us to wisdom beyond our customary grasp, a kind of intellectual alchemy, transmuting the alloy of the mind into the pure gold of enlightenment and truth.

These days when the little shoemaker's shop stood just off the Görlitz Square were, in fact, the days of "renaissance alchemism," a philosophical alchemism, which had come out of the Middle Ages refined and purified and which taught that it was no less a miracle to change a sinner into a saint than it was to produce gold from a base metal or to change an acorn into an oak. If a transmutation can take place in man, it was argued, it can take place in things, and the other way around. The intriguing text of the alchemists was, "Within everything is the seed of everything." As the microcosm man reflects the entire universe, so a drop of water reflects the nature of the sea, a grain of sand the nature of the earth, and every particle of dust and air the nature of the cosmos.

All these things, and deeper things than these, the shoemaker knew and, as I have said, though he was my age in body, he was a thousand and more years older in mind. Here I was, frantically searching. There he sat smiling, carving a piece of leather with his skiver held in steady hands, or humming a half-forgotten song as he lock-stitched the black-pitched threads through the punched-out seams, musing meanwhile that shoes like faith should be tailored to fit life's journey, and that it was perfectly understandable that pilgrims had different lasts.

One day it was rumored that he himself had become a journeyman, a wandering shoemaker. I was told he had left the warmth and comfort of the shop, had turned the key in his vine-covered cottage, and had said adieu to Görlitz. It was true enough. I felt it the moment I entered the shop and saw the proprietor exasperatedly breaking in a new apprentice. He admitted that his former one had advised him he was leaving, but he had refused to believe it. Why would anyone want to leave the village square? And what was this talk about having to "be about my Father's business"? It was still shoe business, wasn't it? "There is no rhyme or reason to things in the world," moaned the proprietor, and he was sure that things would go from bad to worse with him no less than with the journeyman.

"When thou art quiet and still . . ."

As for the local clergy, they thought it was good riddance. The shoemaker, they informed me, had frequently set forth some most heretical doctrines, chief among which was the contention that, "It is possible that when thou art quiet and still and cease thinking of self, that thou wilt hear and see that which God saw and heard in thee." Heretics had been killed for less than this, the pastors reminded me, and I knew that they were quite right. But in fantasy I found myself walking thoughtfully, after my day's chores were done, with the words singing in my heart, "When thou art quiet and still . . . thou wilt hear and see that which God saw and heard in thee." And in my mind's eye I envisioned the wandering shoemaker touching and changing lives through the alchemy of his profound but casual wisdom as he sat in a customer's yard or made himself comfortable in a corner of a house quietly mending shoes.

Reports filtered in that philosophers occasionally took note of him in Dresden, Berlin, Zittau, Halle; spoke with him and walked away reflecting on his knowledge and insight. Once in a while a politician or a landowner had occasion to hear his words while waiting for a boot or a shoe to be mended, and they interrogated him on the practical aspect of his points of view and for the logical meaning these might have for influencing the times in which they lived, for these were the years when Europe was girding itself for one of the biggest and bloodiest religious wars that the world had ever seen, a war that was to last for thirty years.

At that, it was a pertinent question: what is the good of intuitionalism in the light of historic facts? Was a Carpenter able to stop Tiberius Caesar or hold back a Herod or a Titus by affirming, "Now are you the Sons of God"? or "Love your enemies"? or "Ye are the salt of the earth"? Was He able, in fact, to save Himself? Obviously not, and I found it quite discouraging until something told me, almost intuitively, that no one would ever have remembered a Tiberius Caesar or a Herod or a Titus, but for Him. And the march of one lone Figure up a hill changed the world more than all the armies of Rome had ever done and more than the war of thirty years would ever do.

Soon some of the shoemaker's writings began to appear, anonymously at first and then under his name: Jacob Boehme; writings which claimed that good can be known only through contrast with evil, and that life must involve a unity of the conflict of opposites in our nature.

The writings were hard to come by because his books were immediately destroyed if they fell into the hands of the clergy and were condemned and banned and argued against by many a pulpiteer. "What good can come out of Görlitz?" became a stock phrase; and the frequent cry, "Is not this the shoemaker's apprentice?" rang through the countryside.

It got to be an open secret that Boehme had been influenced—and corrupted, it was said—by an earlier heretic, Paracelsus, who had been misguided by an earlier one, Pythagoras, who had been led astray by another named Plato. It was not a clear line that led to Boehme, but his heresy was crystal clear: he related these men to the Carpenter and the Carpenter to himself, and not to himself only, but to everyman, and not only to everyman, but to nature and to life and death and to the universe itself.

"If you will behold your own self and the outer world and what is taking place therein," he wrote, "you will find that you, with regard to your external being, are that external world. You are a little world formed out of the large one, and your external light is a chaos of the sun and the constellations of stars. If this were not so you would not be able to see by means of the sun's light. Not I, the I that I am, know these things, but God in me knows them."

All of this was interesting enough, but one evening after the streets of Görlitz were still, I was rewarded with an encounter considerably more interesting. Near a street lamp not far from *Frauen Kirche,* I saw a freely walking figure, his paraphernalia on his back like an ordinary journeyman, his same easygoing, casual manner giving the impression that life was in divine order and time was on his side. *Mütze* on his head almost jauntily, his bearded face a study in silhouette, he paused to adjust his pack. Point-blank I said, "To read your words, Herr Boehme, is difficult, but to live them is more so."

The angel within man

With a sigh of amused resignation, he replied in his feeble but buoyant tone, "I have trouble on that score myself."

"This matter of intuition," I began, "what is it?"

"The inner whispering of Self," he answered, as if surprised that men should not know this. "Or would you rather call it the voice of God? Oh well, it is no matter. Reason is the mind's mortal understanding of the illumined understanding of the spiritual man. Intuition is the communication between these two unfolding natures."

He called the Self the angel-in-man. Socrates had called it his daemon. Hermes had referred to it as his overman. Jesus had spoken of it as His Father. Herr Boehme was of the opinion that no matter what name it bore, it worked its wonder in some mysterious but natural way and put man into oneness with all men of similar experience and with God.

Spurred on by boldness, I asked, "Isn't this Self also instant knowledge? Isn't it actually what the Psalmist referred to when he said, 'If any man lack understanding, let him ask of God'?"

The shoemaker looked at me with a sudden, strange light of wonder and concern, gave his pack a slight adjusting jolt of his stooped shoulders, and said, "Each man is the Psalmist, don't you see?" With this he touched my hand and walked away.

I stood beneath the light as his shadow merged into the shadows of the street. He went away, but I had the uncanny feeling that he never truly left me, even though a few moments later I heard the sound of the key as he unlocked and opened his cottage door. I walked home then, meditating on the "whispering of Self." The following morning I was told that he had been seen leaving the village before dawn.

Before I saw him again he had already been stripped of his shoemakership and had become a legend, as long ago in Galilee the Carpenter was robbed of His human nature, His struggles, and His quest. Not that Boehme and the Galilean were on an equal level, far from it, and the shoemaker would have been the first to admit this fact. But for his little niche in time, he, in his way, was aware of the commonly unheard and sought to live as though the Voice was real.

Many considered any such conclusion the greatest heresy of all, but others took a stand equally extreme, as I realized one autumn afternoon when my fantasy led me to a group of people who were converting the old shoeshop into a shrine. The mystic had died, I was told, and my informer added, "It is a shame, too, he was barely fifty and had no easy time of it. But, then, he was not an ordinary man by any means."

"Wasn't he?" I asked.

"Lord, no! Didn't you hear how he got his wisdom? Well, I must tell you. You see, he was alone in the shop one day when a stranger came in to buy a pair of shoes. 'How much is this pair?' he asked. Jacob said, 'I do not know the price for my master who handles that end of the business is not here at the moment.' 'Well,' said the stranger, 'if *you* were to put a price on them, how much would it be?' Jacob named a figure and said, 'That is what I would say is a fair price, and my master is a fair man.' Well, the stranger bought the shoes and left. But when he was outside, he suddenly called in a loud voice, 'Jacob! Jacob Boehme, come forth!' Jacob ran out wondering what had happened and then he realized that the stranger was actually an angel, a real, honest-to-goodness angel who took his hand and said, 'Jacob, thou art little but thou shalt be great! Thou shalt be another Man such as to whom the world will stand in wonder!"

"Are you sure it was an angel?" I asked. "Could it not merely have been his thoughts, his wishes, his hope, perhaps? Could it not have been his intuition?"

"Lord, no! It was an angel, I tell you, straight from heaven! A man can't become really good or great without a miracle like that. God chooses these people, don't you know? And the rest of us, well, we're just the rest of us, that's all."

And he hurried away to help drape the altar in the new shrine and to lay a yellow rosebud near the candle holder on the white cloth, while others brought pictures of angels surrounding the shoulders of a man who carried a luminous shoemaker's pack.

Later, in the village square, they put up a statue of Jacob Boehme at great expense and with great ceremony, and they said that Görlitz had no reason to believe that such a one would ever appear again in that part of the world. He had been a special messenger, they said, a chosen one. "And the rest of us? Well, we're just the rest of us, that's all."

And as I watched I thought I heard a shoemaker weeping over a city.

VIII * RECEPTIVITY

They call it receptivity.

They contend that if one is willing to be a clear and open channel for the reception of impressions, it is possible to hear the commonly unheard, by which they mean "spirit Voices," or what they prefer to call "discarnate entities."

I reserved the right to doubt. Even though my informants were highly reputable individuals and friends of mine, all were spiritualistically inclined. They all had a wish to believe, and not a wish only but a will to believe as well.

That life holds unfathomed dimensions was something I could not question. That there are sounds beyond the range of physical hearing could be proved by the simple demonstration of blowing the "silent whistle" with which I summoned my dog. He could hear the whistle's sound but I could not. The vibrations were beyond me. In an ascending scale there were even more sharp-eared or otherwise highly sensitized creatures than dogs which responded to sounds that I know nothing about, and whenever I contemplated some of these facts my mind went roaming.

Take for example the uncanny hearing sense of the nocturnal moth. Here is a fragile, powdery insect that seems no more intelligent than a piece of confetti blown into the breeze. Yet, according to recent scientific studies, these tiny fragments of invertebrate life have such a phenomenal audio apparatus that they not only hear the commonly unheard but depend upon their super-acoustic prowess for their very existence. They can actually hear the ultrasonic beep of a bat which is as sophisticated a sound as can be found anywhere in the animal kingdom and which has never been directly heard by any human ear.

We can detect the screech and clicking noises of bats, but their phantom cries by which they are guided in their pitch-black flights, the "electronic" impulses by which they locate their prey, particularly moths, are simply not heard by humans. But the flimsy moth can hear them and tries to save itself by getting out of the way of the lethal, kamikaze plunges of their winged-mouse predators. Furthermore, for whatever it is worth, the male moth can hear or smell or sense a female moth a mile away and can at this distance determine whether or not it is a virgin.

Every hunter knows that by imitating mating calls he can decoy an animal to its death—a vicious practice but justified even by most Christian Nimrods. Yet, some animals cannot be decoyed because human hunters with all their crafty skills have not been able to decode or duplicate the supersonic love calls of birds and beasts whose language is beyond our range of receptivity.

Breaking through to the spirit worlds

But if a zoologist can invade the world of moths, why cannot a spiritualist break through the veil of spirit worlds? Why did I shy away from the theory presented by my psychic-minded friends that there are individuals who can communicate with "intelligences" on the "other side" and who have "guides" and "controls" and all sorts of other connections beyond the range of my receptive sense?

If they had simply said, "Be open and receptive," that would have been fair enough, but I had the feeling they wanted me to be a full-fledged follower along the seance trail.

I made my position clear. I did have an unbounded curiosity about these things and, I assumed, an open mind. Perhaps I even had a wish and a will to believe but did not want to admit this publicly. I was all for being mystically minded, too, and by mystical I meant that which has a reality not apparent to the senses or obvious to the intelligence. Secretly I often found myself in agreement with the old patriarch Tertullian, who once confessed, "I believe because it is absurd!" But was not this the kind of reasoning a person kept to himself? That a transmarginal realm of consciousness existed was as obvious to me as that a moth had wings, or ears, for that matter, but I was sufficiently receptive to my own intuition to know that if I ever boasted about being a mystic, in that instant my mysticism would disappear. I was sure of that. And the moment I said, "I believe in spirit communication!" that would be the starting point for doubt.

I was all for having my guardian angels and my leprechauns and even my poltergeists, but they were mine and mine alone, created in the image of my receptivity, and if I ever treated them as if they were public domain, they would desert me sure enough.

Who, after all, is not receptive? Who does not have his talismen and portents which he cherishes, and his oafs and spooks which cherish him? Who has not felt the nearness of unseen presences during the free and friendly moments of his solitude? Who has not been receptive to an inner response during periods of great joy or sorrow or when, for no apparent reason, he felt that life was good, that time was kind, and that God was truly on his side?

Of course we have these feelings. They are never far from us. The complex world cannot hide them and the whirring traffic of life cannot crowd them out.

Sometime, as an experiment, listen to your thoughts as you listen to music. Hear within yourself the symphony of impressions, the harmony of ideas, the melodies which in your moments of reflection you are inspired to create and express. We are too much with others and not enough with ourselves. We are drawn away from our true receptivity by too many extraneous sounds. Take time to listen to the thoughts within yourself and when you go back into the crowd your world will be less discordant and your life more perfectly attuned, especially to those who like you have been receptive to their innermost thoughts.

I always had a curiosity about the Biblical accounts of clairaudient powers. When, for example, Scripture says that "A voice came to Samuel," or "There was a voice out of Heaven," what form did these voices take? Were they audible to the physical ear or was there some inner listening post that registered the communications?

After all, how do we get ideas and inspirations? We are fed by an influx of "voices" continually, something is always speaking to us, giving us new thoughts, big thoughts, oftentimes wild and unreasonable thoughts so that we stand in amazement and ask, "Where did *that* come from?" The joy and wonder of life consist not only in looking at the ordinary things in an extraordinary way but in listening to the inner promptings with special expectation. Many religious groups have a saying, "When man listens, God speaks." If this is not spirit communication, my friends insisted, what is? In fact, they went so far as to say that heaven is not really real unless you believe in communication not only with the Spirit of God but with the spirits of loved ones who have passed on. And, to pursue the matter further, they claimed that unless heaven *is* real, this present earth life will remain shallow and limited.

Such reasoning bothered me for I was continually meeting happy, well-integrated, well-intentioned people who apparently did not believe in the hereafter one bit. There was, for example, a man with a most wholesome outlook on life who agreed with Lin Yutang that too much contemplation about the dead and dying is pathological. This man used to say, "Live your best because this is your one chance to make life worth-while."

He once wrote to me, "Don't waste your time on some faraway heaven where you think you will live the way you *could* live right now by right thinking. *This* is your life. Everybody is waiting for a day when he can start life with a clean slate. But every *moment* is a new starting and every turn of the mind can wipe the slate clean for a new beginning."

He truly tried to live this way. The good he felt he should do was done as faithfully as time allowed. Decisions were made with a minimum waste of effort and time. Every day *was* for him a new challenge and he was playing his part to the full because he felt that when the curtain came down, "my show will be over."

I did not agree with him in his apparent belief that death ends all, but many times I wished with all my heart that I had his courage to live my present life as fully and as well as he lived his. With all my faith in a future life I was no better off than he with faith in none of it. I have no idea how he will meet death when it comes, but I have a hunch that in the final act he will very likely say to himself, "Well, now, let's see what we can make of this with a minimum of fuss and waste of time."

But to live only to be destroyed at the close of life, to believe that death means the end of all consciousness, all experiences, memories, and creative continuity, these were assumptions I had to deny because of my receptivity to God's good. My "inner voices" denied such finalities. Something told me that annihilation was unreal, unfair, and unlike God as I imagined Him to be. Why would He make the "show of life" a one-act play and bring the curtain down without an encore? Which always brought me back to the interesting speculation of my psychic friends, "If consciousness lives apart from the body, is it not possible to make *contact*, especially through those who have unusual psychic receptivity?"

Jessie Eubank's office

Among the most unusual psychic-receptives whose paths crossed mine was Arthur Ford. He had an autobiographical book, *Nothing So Strange*. He had a luminous history, having "broken" the code which Houdini had left to be deciphered after his passing. He had credentials, having been ordained in the Disciples of Christ denomination and having demonstrated his prowess to a long list of important people. Most of all, he had a friendly, easygoing way about this matter of psychism and I had heard him discuss his view at Union Theological Seminary, at Riverside Church in New York, in college classrooms, and in my home where he occasionally consented to meet small groups of questing people.

Like most sensitives, he had a "control" or a "spirit go-between" who purportedly spoke through him during the moments when he

(Ford) was in a trancelike sleep. This invisible guide, Fletcher by name, identified himself as a discarnate who had lived and died a short century ago and who now from the spirit realm had discovered in Ford a perfect channel for psychic demonstrations.

Such was the story and usually at the Ford sessions revealing and provocative "messages" came through via Fletcher. Frequently there were highly veridical communications as, for example, when Fletcher announced to me, "There is a woman here (in spirit) who comes to say that you will be taking a trip into Missouri. She says you will be using an office that once was hers."

"What is her name?" I asked.

"Jessie Eubank," was the reply.

Since the name was unfamiliar to me I asked the other members in our circle of fourteen if they had ever heard of a Jessie Eubank. No one had any knowledge of her.

"Jessie Eubank," I asked, "how did you die?"

The reply came through "Fletcher" who, speaking through Ford, said, "She was killed in an automobile accident."

Before I could ask for more details, "Fletcher" was off on other matters, bringing various messages to other persons in the room.

Now a trip to Missouri was on my schedule, but neither Ford nor anyone in the circle could possibly have known about it. My itinerary was incomplete and when I made the trip several weeks later it included a number of stops, with a final lecture assignment at Stephens College, Columbia.

I had all but forgotten our psychic session when I reached Columbia, but on the evening of my arrival I was invited to the home of the college president, Dr. Seymour Smith. He had asked several faculty members in for a buffet supper. During the conversation, Dr. Smith casually remarked, "By the way, while you are here with us you may, if you wish, use Jessie Eubank's office for consultations."

For a moment the name did not register. Then it emerged incredibly in my mind as I recalled our evening of "communication with the dead." I must have looked at Dr. Smith half-amused and half-astonished, for he was prompted to ask, "Have you heard of her?"

"As a matter of fact," I said, "I heard of Jessie Eubank for the first time several weeks ago. In a psychic session."

"In a what?" asked one of the men.

"You might call it an experiment in receptivity," I said. "By the way, how did Jessie Eubank die?"

"She was killed," said one of the guests, "in an automobile accident."

The tantalizing quest

We discussed the tantalizing question of "spirit communication" under the general heading of parapsychological phenomena, although even that title did not make the subject academically acceptable. We hazarded guesses whether it is conceivable that a veil as deep and timeless as that which separates the living from the dead can be drawn aside by the simple process of a "sensitive" dropping into a self-imposed, hypnotic sleep, commonly referred to as a trance. If consciousness does survive after death, can certain psychics like Ford "tune in?" Do "Fletchers" really exist on "the other side" or are they merely the medium's alter-ego, his own psyche dipping into the pool of conscious or unconscious thought created by those who sit in the seance circles?

As I thought about these things, I remembered how many evidential messages I had recorded in psychic sessions across the country and in various parts of the world; how once in the Guatemalan mountains near Chichicastenango a Mayan medium told me that a voice informed him that my mother was very ill, a report which I verified the following day; how on another occasion I put test questions to an "entity" that had identified herself as my departed sister and found the answers amazingly correct. Even messages that at the time sounded like trivia later took on telltale signs of an intimate knowledge of family affairs.

Perhaps there *are* highly sensitized individuals and there is certainly a good chance that there are degrees of development in receptivity just as there are in musical, artistic, or other innate talents.

No one put the matter into a more gentle parable than did Louis K. Anspacher, a psychical researcher, in his *Challenge of the Unknown:* "Consider," he said, "the biological phenomenon called histolysis. . . . A caterpillar winds itself in its cocoon, its chrysalis. The cocoon serves to isolate and insulate the caterpillar from natural selection and from any necessity of adaptation to its environment. Then inside of this cocoon occurs the amazing, stupefying process called histolysis. All the larval organs disappear. All the organs of the caterpillar are reduced to an amorphous, formless jelly, a sort of viscous emulsion, having no discernible structure. Then, by some miracle of reorganization, directed by some mysterious dynamism, energized by some obscure force, this formless and apparently dead emulsion transforms itself into the complete insect, a butterfly. . . .

"Now let us imagine a supernormal, queer caterpillar, or, if you like, a caterpillar gifted with psychic powers, meeting an ordinary caterpillar. Imagine this psychic caterpillar trying to explain histolysis to the skeptical, common-sense, club-man caterpillar enjoying the cabbages of this world's garden. What would the common-sense club-man caterpillar reply to the psychic caterpillar? He'd say 'Oh yeah, sure! That's all right if you like to believe it. But as far as my observation goes, this jolly, conscious life of mine ends with my coffin, the cocoon. . . . So, permit me, please permit me to enjoy my cabbages.'"

Yet no one better than the gifted Anspacher knew that the tantalizing quest for knowledge of and communication with the unknown are the common impulse of every man, be he supernormal or club-man type. Every last one of us has his moments of receptivity and his experiences when he hears the commonly unheard and sees the commonly unseen. Clear or clouded inner voices, impulses, and hunches come to all of us, happen to all of us, without our making them happen. Only we best know how far we should go in this field and how much credence we should attach to these experiences. Only we know—and sometimes not even we can be quite sure what forces and powers are at work in us when we are open and receptive.

An almost-unbelievable story

I had an unforgettable meeting with jeweler Albert Perrones who enjoys the confidence of a highly respectable city clientele. He had been alone in his Detroit store one day shortly before closing time when a smartly dressed, attractive woman came in, laid her white gloves and her overly large purse on the showcase and explained that an insurance company had just reimbursed her in the amount of $2500 for the loss of a precious engagement ring. This money, she said, she wished to reinvest in another diamond. "The sentiment," she observed with a sigh, "can never be replaced, but I do want to get another stone as good as the one dear Jim gave me."

Perrones set a velvet tray of quality diamonds on the showcase. "Yes," he agreed, "there are some things money cannot buy." She looked him straight in the eye and said, "Diamonds have something spiritual about them."

Perrones was pleased. "My father used to say," he told her, "that the brightest stars are diamonds that God gave to His best angels."

The woman laughed good-naturedly at this and then suddenly put her hand to her forehead. "My," she said, "it is very warm. I feel quite faint."

Perrones asked if she would like a glass of water and, impelled by his own suggestion, went to the water dispenser just recently installed in the back room of the store. It was not until he returned a moment later, glass in hand, that the quick start and take-off of a car shocked him into realizing his unsuspecting guilelessness. His customer was gone, along with purse and gloves and the diamond-studded tray.

He set the glass of water thoughtfully on the showcase. What surprised him most was that he had no desire to dash out in pursuit of the woman or call the police. Instead he found himself in a strange philosophical frame of mind. True, the diamonds were covered by insurance. Equally true was the fact that he was chagrined at his gullibility after nearly thirty years in the business, but something deeper and more inexplicable caused him to stand silently, gazing at the spot where the tray had been. What he seemed to see there was God giving the brightest diamonds to His best angels. In some way the vision was more real than the diamonds had been. And just as he was thinking that he had never felt this way before, he heard a voice, or at least he thought he heard a voice that said, "They are not really gone."

He explained to me that the words were "like a whisper in my mind" and that he was by no means given to voices or psychic experiences or anything of the kind. The words, however, were so persuasive and seemed to him so right that he placed his hands on the showcase where the diamonds had been and repeated earnestly and aloud, "You're right, Lord. They are not really gone."

Throughout the night the conviction hung on that this had not been a wishful illusion but, rather, an omen of good. He was convinced that he was involved in a drama not of his making and in an interlude rich with some hidden meaning.

When he stepped inside his store the following morning he was hardly surprised to see the tray of diamonds on the shining glass top of the showcase. It was there complete and unaltered, bearing its same authentic merchandise. He stood there nodding understandingly, wondering at what risk this precarious loot had been returned. How had it been returned? Why? No matter.

Who would believe his story? Only those who knew him. They believed it. Only someone like I who had often been tempted to say with old Tertullian, "I believe because it is so absurd. I believe because it transcends my reason"; as the moth transcends my reason, and the bat, and my dog, and many other marvelous wonders of nature's most marvelous world.

I keep telling myself that as far as receptivity is concerned, there is no greater measure of it in others than in me. There is no greater awareness of it in others than in me. There is no more power, understanding, or ability to hear the commonly unheard in others than in me; the only difference is that some in turning their receptivity of these qualities upon themselves do not despise them or cheapen them or run them through a mill of doubt and incredulity.

After all, where does credulity end and incredulity begin? It is a personal matter and we judge it according to our power of receptivity. The more a man knows, the more he hears. The wider his knowledge, the greater his world. "As long as we deal with the cosmic and the general," said William James, "we deal only with the symbols of reality, but as soon as we deal with private and personal phenomena we deal with realities in the completest sense of the term. That unsharable feeling which each of us has of the pinch of his individual destiny, as he privately feels it rolling out of fortune's wheel, may be disparaged for its egotism, may be sneered at as unscientific, but it is the one thing that fills up the measure of our concrete actuality, and any would-be existence that lacks such a feeling would be a piece of reality only half made up. . . . A bill of fare with one real raisin on it instead of the word "raisin," with one real egg instead of the word "egg," might be an inadequate meal, but it would at least be the commencement of reality."

I cannot say that I have ever learned to tune in to the commonly unheard. I have not even become adept at putting aside a specific time or period for some psychic rendezvous, but often at unexpected moments the nearness of vibrations from some other realm are received rather effortlessly, and a sense of guidance gives the hint of other lively worlds close to my own.

Sometimes when I summon my dog and give him commands via the silent whistle in which he hears his master's voice, I cannot help but wonder about the Voice or voices unheard by others but which, at times, seem to be commanding me.

PART THREE

THE COMMONLY UNFELT

IX • EMPATHY

Faith is a feeling. Faith is empathy with the unknown.

I became convinced of this early in my research when for no apparently logical reason I found myself guided time and again by an inner force, as if something or someone were taking the initiative for me and quietly but surely directing my way. I know what the Mandalay monk meant when he asked, "What do you feel when you feel the commonly unfelt?"

Dependence upon this feeling of guidance required courage while at the same time the courage intensified the feeling. It was a circular operative approach. Faith, I had to conclude, does not reach its full potential until it has been tried, but there is a reluctance to try it until its potential has been proved. It is up to the doer to take the first courageous step and start the experiment.

As I look back on the development of this in my own experience, I realize that guidance works best if I give it a light touch, a playful, mimetic quality which can be construed as either faith or folly depending upon the point of view.

The touch of St. Anthony

Take the matter of finding a parking space. When the city I live in boomed its way to greatness a few years ago, we motorists were battling it out every hour of the day haunted by the realization that in our great, wide, beautiful, wonderful world it was now necessary to lie in wait or prowl the streets to find twelve small feet of cemented ground which had not already been usurped. About this time an enterprising friend told me about St. Anthony, solemnly assuring me that his parking problem had been solved by appealing directly to this fourth-century saint. "Strange thing," he confided, "but parking spots open up magically when the good saint and I are *en rapport.*"

I did not believe a word of it, of course, but on the other hand I believed it implicitly, for it always seemed to me that if life does not have an overtone of mystery and game-ism, living is a cold, impersonal assignment, to say the least, and if a man ever loses his childlike feeling for the unseen he is in truly desperate straits. Every last one of us still carries with him the dreams and make-believe of his youth and feels his nearness to them as he plays his part on the overcrowded stage of life.

The truth of the matter was that I had always had a special intimate feeling for St. Anthony, though I am not a Catholic, and I said to myself, "If St. Antonius works for my friend, how much more will he work for me if I but let my needs be known, needs like parking spots, for example."

The uninitiated will scarcely understand this and the cold-headed intellectual will understand it not at all, but for those who have the will-to-believe, it will immediately become part of the game. It is not an attempt to turn a saint into a servitor in the ordinary sense of the word; it is more a matter of awakening within oneself a slumbering faith factor, a feeling that it is possible to know when and where unseen help and guidance may be expected. It boils down to a kind of soliloquizing with oneself, a subtlety in which, for a little while, we confess to ourselves depths of feeling we believe in for ourselves alone, and in which we deny the very spirit of the game if we try to urge these feelings and beliefs upon anyone else. We start with little things, inconsequentials—like parking spaces—and soon we find that the technique can be employed in things of consequence.

To come back to St. Anthony. Because of my affection for this Egyptian-born mystic, I had purchased de Voragine's *Golden Leg-*

end long before I comprehended the deeper meaning of the myths. I liked the ribald Antonius because he had the light touch. Once, when asked about the secret of salvation, he said, "If anyone strikes you on the right cheek, do as the Master said and turn the other also."

His hearers replied, "That is beyond our ability."

"Well," said Anthony, "then at least be patient when you are struck on one cheek."

"That is still beyond us," they murmured.

"Dear me," said Anthony with a sigh, "then at least be content not to strike back."

"Even that is more than we can do," they told him.

At this, Anthony turned to one of his followers and said, "Mix a drink for these brethren, for in truth they are exceedingly feeble and need support!"

Of course, he had his serious side. He was persuaded that God and the Devil were vying for the souls of men and he was always getting himself involved in this struggle on the Lord's side. A number of times he invited martyrdom from those who despised the Christians or who thought him overly superstitious, but when he reached the age of 100, he told his friends that God would give him five more years for good measure, which was exactly what God did.

At the age of twenty he had given away a sizable family inheritance to the less fortunate. As was customary in those days, he became a hermit and attracted followers who wanted not money but secrets to live by. Eventually he started five monastic orders to suit the needs and temperaments of those who followed various occupations and who had a fervent feeling for the commonly unfelt.

After his death he became a patron saint of various professions, all the way from gravediggers to hospital attendants. In his name, people experienced healing miracles, recovered lost articles, and walked and talked with the spiritual presence of Antonius, who evidently kept himself within easy reach of the most lowly. The only credential anyone needed to get his support was a believing heart.

I often go into liturgical churches to light a candle to friend Anthony and to whisper a prayer that every man might find God according to his understanding, and I according to mine. It is, as I have said, a game without pretense or theological collusion of any kind; as simple as belief in the presence of a loved one or in the sights and sounds of Christmas, it is a feeling and, when harmonized with belief, things begin to happen.

I remember one day when it was imperative for me to park in a particularly busy section of town. While still a quarter of a mile away I began my soliloquy to my unseen friend. Almost immediately I felt the overpowering sense of assurance that a place would be waiting for me in the exact block where I needed to go. I had gone through this feeling process often enough absolutely to *know when I knew* that a good contact had been established.

This time, however, I arrived at my appointed place only to find cars parked airtight up and down every available lane. All I could do was drive by, and as I did so I heard myself say aloud, "It simply isn't possible to feel a thing so strongly and not have it happen!" But the circumstances belied my words. Then I glanced into my rear-view mirror and lo and behold a car pulled out behind me as if the saint himself had suddenly swooped down and taken the wheel. Also, as if by design, the street was momentarily clear, allowing me to back up and get into the place just vacated, exactly in front of the establishment where I needed to go.

Could feeling be more real than seeing?

Do I believe it? I do absolutely and I don't. By which I mean, I do when I have the feeling and when the game is right, but I do not fully understand the process nor would I say how much saintly intervention is involved! Furthermore, there is always the annoying question about what happens to the other person who needs the parking space fully as much as I and who finds me just moving in! And what would Antonius do if more people needed spaces than the block provided? There is an old, nagging question, "If you thank God for saving your life, what about those whose lives are not saved?" Is it possible that good fortune and success are accruable only to those who have the basic feeling for possessing these virtues? Can it be that the things which the eyes do not see, the soul must feel, and that the feeling is more real than the seeing?

This much I know. There are moments of attunement, and the more we develop and trust our inner awareness, the more operative the awareness becomes, and if there is mystery involved in this, very well, there is mystery. We must be true to our capacity to respond and we should, by rights, be conscious of our sensitivity to experiences from beyond the so-called transmarginal reaches of the mind.

What do you see when you look at a rose? What do you hear when you listen to the wind? And what do you feel when you feel the commonly unfelt?

Why, after all, did a monk in Mandalay ask these questions of me or permit me to sit with him through several days of discussion when his own time was at a premium? There is an easy answer but a mysterious one: empathy. I knew beyond the shadow of a doubt that I would see this monk even as I walked alone and unannounced to his retreat without the benefit of appointment. I simply knew, just as I once knew with the same kind of certainty, that I would be permitted to see the noted stigmatist, Theresa Neumann, in Konnersreuth, Germany, although the taxi driver who grudgingly drove me over the icy kilometers said, "I have taken better people than you to see this woman and they didn't get in. What makes you think you are different?"

I wasn't different. I was guided.

Empathy.

Empathy is a feeling. I rather think it is first of all an awareness that everyone is on a quest. This may be the heart of it. Perhaps most of the world's ills could be solved by an understanding of this single, solitary thought. The quest can mean no single discovery. It involves a combination of discoveries, an instrumentation in itself, but symphonic in unison, especially when the Master of the quest wields the baton.

This realization constituted the most notable changing point in my life. I never had an answer for the whims and caprices of myself or others until I understood the questing quality of life. Only then did my own predilections become clear. Only then was I able to see with reason the solicitudes of those whose lives touched mine. This, in fact, became the very heart of my work and research; I discovered an ultimate philosophy in the concept that the search is an equivalent for the discovery. The moment you begin to seek, you have already found, for you have set your feet upon the path, and this is basic whether it is a parking space you seek or God. Faith is a feeling. An empathy.

The passkey

We are all alike in that we are interrelated in a search for meaning in life, but as searchers we are all different. I may, at times, play the game with St. Antonius while you may want a guardian angel or a hunch or even a rabbit's foot. We are all different, but we are all alike. When William James observed how souls found their fulfillment in the universe of his time a half century ago, he concluded that "if an Emerson were forced to be a Wesley, or a Moody were forced to be a Whitman, the total human consciousness of the divine would suffer." Just so in our day if a Sartre, let us say, were compelled to be a Barth, or a Billy Graham were forced to be a Paul VI, contemporary religion would be reduced considerably and the expression of faith would be notably impaired. It is not uniformity we need, but understanding, not tolerance, but insight, not points of view, but points of connection, not appraisal, but *empathy*, the ability to feel the commonly unfelt, and when we begin to practice this virtue we instantly widen our world.

Wherever I have gone among cultural and ethnic groups during my global circuit-riding, I have depended upon three infallible and popular convictions: 1. There is nothing which anyone experiences on the feeling level that I cannot also experience; 2. The quest of every individual regardless of his cultural pattern is similar to mine; 3. The sincerity of my quest is sensed by others just as I sense the degree of their sincerity in them.

This approach is the passkey that permits me to enter many seemingly impenetrable groups, all groups, in fact, with the possible exception of the Black Muslims. These followers of Prophet Poole ruled me out because I am white. But even though they barred me from their services, they were ready and willing to sit down with me and discuss their beliefs, a potpourri of ancient Islam and a modern revolt against the white world of our time. They will learn, as all groups do eventually, and as the followers of the late Father Divine have already remarkably demonstrated, that without empathy we remain confined to a restricted arc in the total circumference of life and fail ever to grasp the full circle of the adventurous quest.

The Black Muslims ruled me out, but the "white Moslems"—that is the people of Islam—ruled me in. I remember climbing to the minaret of a Syrian mosque in a village not far from Damascus, there to stand with the muezzin when he gave his call to prayer: "*La illah illa'llah! Mohammed rasulu'llah!*" (There is no God but Allah! Mohammed is His Prophet!)

It was Friday, the Moslem Sabbath, and the muezzin was saying, "Hasten to prayer! Hasten to prayer!" The call reached back to the days of Mohammed, who captivated the sixth-century world with a new religion that was not really new. It was eclectic, borrowing from and contributing to the sources from which it drew its strength, Judaism, Christianity, and Oriental philosophies.

The black-robed muezzin stood like a figure spun out of an ancient tapestry. Through cupped hands he sent the call backward and forward in time and space. I had the vivid feeling that I had lived through the entire history and aspiration of his people since first their faith began. I was the farmer who paused in his field beyond the minaret. I was the workman who listened on the dusty road. I was the merchant in the doorway of his shop turning in the direction of the holy city of Mecca Hijaz. I was the child who halted in his running as he heard the muezzin call, and the woman who stopped thoughtfully with the water jar balanced on her head. I was the worshiper who made his ablutions in the courtyard of the mosque, removed his shoes, and knelt on the prayer rug with his forehead to the ground. Somewhere, somehow, I had seen it all before.

Why should this seem strange, I asked myself, when I had the identical feeling in Israel in Jewish synagogues and while I walked the streets of Tel Aviv and the roads of new Jerusalem? When I heard the rabbis read from the sacred scrolls, "Hear, O Israel, the Lord our God, the Lord is One!" it could have been my voice that did the reading. When they bowed their covered heads over the holy pages in that hushed moment when the troubled land was still, it was not at all strange for me to feel that I stood with them, or to imagine that my lips touched and tasted the honey on the scroll. The bearded patriarch of orthodoxy, the spirited young worker in the kibbutz, the child at his quest, I had the feeling that I had been through these experiences in some well-remembered past.

I felt the same way when I walked with the Buddhists in Sarnath, India, where the Buddha walked. They saw a vision of their master and I, through them, saw mine, while sometimes because of each other we were better able to see our own. The feeling persisted that, long before I visited with Buddhist monks in their monasteries in Southeast Asia, I had already sat with them at their lighted candles somewhere in the past. I had walked with begging bowl in hand as they did, had learned the doctrine of the Eightfold Path, and had memorized their definition of virtue: Do as little harm as possible, do good in abundance, and seek to practice love, compassion, truthfulness, and purity in all walks of life.

I had been one in spirit with the Hindus, too, long before I ever entered their holy city of Benares or bathed in the waters of the sacred Ganges. So vivid was all this that I was not one bit surprised to hear a Brahman priest say to me one day, "We met here once before." And why not? For that is what empathy does. It turns the world around until we meet again where first our spirits met. Or perhaps it moves the world forward until we meet where we must meet at last.

When I lived for a while among the Ramakrishna monks and sat with them on the floor eating my food with my fingers as they did, it seemed to me as if this had been rehearsed somewhere before in this self-same land. We had many discussions there in Calcutta, but I had the feeling that we were merely picking up the threads of an unfinished conversation which had begun ages ago. Now we were reassembling the bits and pieces which we had pooled when first our talks began. I do not mean reincarnation or transmigration or all the other terms with which we seek to explain the mysteries of empathic union. I mean, rather, that there is a world of brotherhood and spiritual accord so close that we often reach out spontaneously and touch it. But the more we try to hold it the more it refuses to be held. Like a bird in the hand, it cannot be clasped too tightly without destroying it. It is a feeling. An empathy. No one can contrive it or catch it in any man-made net. Even old Antonius knew that.

Humility and understanding

He had a dream one time in which he saw the people of the world covered with nets. Men and women of every nation and culture were caught, enmeshed, imprisoned in the tangle of their lives. Anthony cried out, "Dear God! How can anyone ever escape?" And a voice answered him, saying, "Only by way of humility and understanding."

Humility and understanding—and the light touch. Like finding parking spaces for the fun of it.

Once an archer criticized Antonius for his seeming propensity for joy. Said the archer, "How can you, a man of God, find time and inclination for so much amusement in life?"

Anthony said, "Put in an arrow and arch your bow."

The bowman complied and Anthony asked him to draw back the bow farther and farther until the archer exclaimed, "If I stretch it much more it will break!"

"So it is with life and our service to the Lord," said Anthony. "If we stretch ourselves beyond our measure in our seriousness we, too, will soon be broken. Therefore it is good that we lay aside our severity from time to time."

Ella Wheeler Wilcox made it too easy when she said, "So many paths, so many creeds, so many roads that wind and wind, when just the art of being kind is all this old world needs."

Alfred North Whitehead made it too difficult when he warned us that if we took the spiritual concepts of the Gospel literally we would be inviting "sudden death."

There is a middle way and on it is a guidepost reading, "Empathy!" How it is generated, how it operates, how it is made to work, to all of these concerns we can only say, "Like faith or love, empathy is a feeling."

Theatrical empathy is another thing. It can be contrived and computed, for it is meant only for the moment. An actor, laughing up his sleeve, can make his hearers cry. There are religionists who save others while they themselves are lost. But when the commonly unfelt is truly experienced empathically, nothing has been arranged by either design or deception, and there is nothing that needs doing. It simply is.

People are always saying to me, "You cannot be all things to all men," but it may be that this is but their way of guarding against being anything to anyone. I have had moments when the greater sin would have been to *resist* being all things to all men.

Empathy tells me that the Shintoist who offers his sprig of *Sokaki* and lights his bit of incense is merely re-enacting my practice of placing an offering on the altar and lighting a votive candle. The Parsi, tasting the pungent drops of *nirangdeen*, is but my other self sharing in Communion. The Confucianist standing before his ancestral shrine is my shadow pausing in memory over those responsible for my advent into the world. The animist who beats his drum is my ancient self returning for its moment of ecstasy. All exist for the individual who has the empathy to be united with them for a little while in spirit.

Antonius knew this much better than I, and that is why he became the patron saint for so many from so many walks of life. Perhaps because of this he loves to play the game and help me find a parking spot. I wouldn't ask anyone to believe it unless he knew the secret.

I call it empathy, the ability to feel the commonly unfelt.

X * CONSCIOUSNESS

I am indebted to a medically minded friend of mine for a significant insight into feeling the commonly unfelt. Dr. David Means of Hemet, California, said, "When I have read over a patient's medical questionnaire I sit down with the person and say, 'You have told me how your body feels. How do *you* feel?' "

Psychotherapist Leslie M. LeCron has somewhat the same approach when during questioning sessions with his patients he asks, "Is there a deeper level at which you know you can get over this trouble?"

When I think of the people who come to me for spiritual consultation (the only kind I know anything about), and when I remember what miracles of changed lives have taken place not because of anything I did or said, but merely because of something that was experienced during the moments of meditation and prayer, I would hesitate to put a limit on the therapy of feeling the commonly unfelt. "You have told me how your body feels. How do you feel?" Granted that there are deep-seated psychoses, unconscious emotional disturbances, repressions, and psychical delusions of many kinds, the truth of the matter is that what most of us need, more than anything else, is a realization of how little, not how much, is wrong with us. We need to be reminded that what we often feel as abnormalities are the normal lot of everyone and that we are better off than we think we are, more fortunate than we imagine, and what we have lost is not our grip on things, but our gratitude.

Why not help yourself?

Why do we refuse to count our blessings or insist that life should not have its moments of testing, encounter, or conflict? Why will we not see that trials are turning points urging us to tap our spiritual resources, and that they may be preparations equipping us for handling greater responsibilities?

We give up too easily on ourselves. Something in our culture, many things in our culture, have robbed us of our self-reliance, our deeper awareness, our consciousness of God and good within ourselves. We want to be helped but we do not want to help ourselves. We want to pay someone for something we already have. We want to be coddled, pampered, loved, anything to escape from the transforming power of an inborn resource which is life's innate gift to every last one of its children. We talk about *my* doctor, *my* specialist, *my* analyst, *my* adviser, *my* consultant, *my* counselor, *my* deodorant, and *my* laxative!

I would be more patient with those who suffer from self-willed psychoses if I had not met the ever legendary Helen Keller. Often when I listen to those who feel they have been manhandled by fate, or when I sit with myself during my own moments of dilemma and discontent, the vision of this remarkable woman comes between me and my seemingly troubled self.

There she stands, having none of the sensory faculties for which I should be on my knees in gratitude. Speech, sight, and hearing have been denied her. The words I glibly speak, the scenes I take for granted, the sounds that register in me effortlessly and as matter-of-course impressions are all out of her world. She walks in darkness. She talks with consciously trained sounds. She reads with her fingers. Yet in the cloistered fastness of her life there shines a light brighter than that which shines in me. The thoughts she projects are crystal clear. Her touch is sensitive with a mystical perception. She lives with consciousness, an attribute or condition of the soul, an awareness of the God within, whatever your definition of God may be. Consciousness is her life, her true life, her eternal, unending limitless perception. And consciousness also constitutes the phenomenon of you and me.

We cannot limit it to Helen Keller, for we have seen consciousness expressed in other lives in other ways. In a north Illinois town a boy was born with a birth defect to which doctors gave the long and frightening name myelomeningocele. At age one he underwent surgery and it was discovered that he not only had an incurable spinal defect but also a cancerous growth in his stomach. The doctors said that if he lived he would never walk.

His mother saw what they did not see. She felt what they did not feel. She saw and felt her child walking, even climbing trees, and as she held this vision in her consciousness she diligently massaged the boy's legs every day. In her mind she saw him walk. She saw her health inspiring him, her spirit influencing his, until there came a time, some eighteen months later, when her boy began to move his legs. She continued her treatments, and her feeling of faith increased. Stirred by the consciousness of this intrepid mother, doctors took new interest in the case. The boy began to crawl, then walk, then run, and finally there came a day when, with his brother and sister, he climbed a tree.

When I think of intrepid people of this kind, I ask myself with new meaning, "And how do *you* feel?"

You must stand up to faith if something within you tells you to, and if it does not, you can, if you wish, arouse yourself by an act of will. You must often carry the dream alone. You must believe what consciously you may be tempted to deny because at a deeper level you *feel* a guidance greater than your own. It is no longer a belief, it is a knowing; in fact, it is no longer a knowing, it is an experience. For when the mirror of reflection is turned on your subjective self, consciousness becomes your infallible guide.

See yourself in your nakedness

During my boyhood I listened to my pastor uncle, *Onkel Pfarrer*, preach an explosive sermon on the end of the world. My eight-year-old heart was filled with fright at the fateful warning of Armageddon, a day which, according to my uncle, could burst forth even before we sat down to our Sunday dinners. "Two shall be in the field, the one shall be taken and the other left. Two women shall be grinding at the mill, one shall be taken and the other left. Watch, therefore, for ye know not the hour when the Son of man cometh!"

Hurling these thunderbolts of Matthew at us, the bearded prophet of God in his black robe and blacker *mütze* challenged us to go home and see ourselves in all our nakedness.

I took him literally. Walking in a daze, sneaking furtive glances at heaven, flinching at the thought of my chances against Jehovah, warding off His blows even before the stars began to fall, I went up to my parents' room to the huge adjustable mirror in the towering oak dresser. I took off my clothes, having no idea what I had done to warrant the end of the world, but sure I had done something. Or perhaps I was condemned for not having done anything. At any rate, I saw myself in all my nakedness, but I did not think it was too bad since that was the way God had made me.

Leaning over the dresser until my nose touched the man-sized mirror, I looked into my eyes earnestly for the first time in my life and asked myself the man-sized questions: Who am I? What am I? Why am I? What is this underlying stuff referred to as *me*? Why have I come into the world if all the strikes are against me and if I am unequipped to cope with the fearful power of things?

I stood there long and intently, trying not even to blink, until it seemed as if I was no longer looking into my eyes, eyes were looking at me. I was held there hypnotized and had I known about Meister Eckhart in those days I would probably have said, "The eyes with which I see God are the same eyes with which he sees me." But I did not know about Meister Eckhart. I only know that I stood entranced until I heard a voice behind me. My mother's voice was saying, "What kind of silliness is this! Put your clothes on and get washed. It's time to eat!"

Quietly I turned from the "mirror of reflection," but the experience never left me. Teleological schemata, theoretical argumentation, metaphysical systems have as of today not answered all of my questions or solved all of the mystery. Voices still break into my reveries with the necessary reminder that a man must dress and wash and eat, that Armageddon is still being predicted, and that pulpit-pounding prophets, well intentioned and theologically skilled, are still urging us to see ourselves in "all our nakedness." But at a deeper level of feeling, the probing of the "eyes that look at me" convinces me of a subjective idealism, assuring me that the world I live in and move in, the world which I call "the universe my home," is the result of consciousness and not the cause of it.

Every person is a phenomenon. It was a great day when we learned that we are not victims of a capricious creator or slaves of incomprehensible forces, but free manifestations of a universal, cosmic expression. Emerson said, "God has need of such a person as I." Modern truth teachers, so-called, tell us that, "However humble your place in life, however unknown to the world you may be, however small your capabilities may seem to you, you are just as necessary to God in His efforts to get Himself into visibility as is the most brilliant intellect, the most thoroughly cultured person in the world."

This does not mean that all imponderables have been solved. By no means. My years of research have not yet answered the questions I asked of the mirror of reflection. I still do not know, for example, how or why I happen to be on this particular rung of the evolutionary ladder in this special period in time and space. I have never come to any clear conclusion as to whether this is my first life experience or if I have been here on earth before in previous cycles of physical manifestations. I look for answers in impressions, impulses, inner revelations, telltale signs, and search for them at various levels of feeling as one searches for treasures at various geological levels.

"What is the origin of man?"

Did I evolve from some subhuman substance or was I fashioned full-blown by the "hand of God?" College students bombard me with the same question. A valid reason for our being on earth at all continues to intrigue us even though we now have left the earth and are orbiting about in space. I sit in on discussions on evolution on many university campuses. I listen to lectures and page through metaphysical books. I even try to read Madam Blavatsky's *Secret Doctrine* and Eric Neumann's noble effort, *The Origin and Birth of Consciousness,* based on the theory of the uroboris. In sheer self-defense I often come back to my preacher uncle. After all, I was a straight "A" student when it came to the fundamental questions in our catechetical instruction.

"What is the origin of man?" *Herr Pastor* would ask and my hand was usually the first to be raised. "The answer is recorded in Genesis chapter one, verses twenty-six and twenty-seven. 'And God said, Let us make man in our image, after our likeness: and let them have dominion . . . over all the earth. . . . So God created man in his own image, in the image of God created he him; male and female created he them.'"

I loved the singing quality of it. I liked the rhythm, the challenge it put upon my memory, the solid sense of faith it gave me. There were, of course, several puzzlers, but *Herr Pastor* solved them with a perfunctory wave of his hand and an authoritarian boom of his voice. He explained that when God declared, "Let *us* make man," He had the Trinity in mind. When God said, "Let *them* have dominion," He was referring to both male and female. *Herr Pastor,* schooled in the German tradition, would have liked to believe that woman was an afterthought, but sound exegesis would not allow it. As to the time of man's creation, he was indefinite, but he assumed—according to the calculation of Biblicist Usher's chronology—that it must have been at least 10,000 long years before the coming of the Christian era.

Adroitly he evaded the question whether the image in which man and woman were created was spiritual or physical. I rather think he leaned toward the belief that God was anthropomorphic, a Superman, as *Herr Pastor* himself was something of a super-figure in the community. My acceptance of the spiritual creative theory came slowly but surely. Although of German descent, I was never persuaded that God was German, even though my mother insisted that the only effective way to pray was in the German language, which was also the way my father felt about swearing.

Despite my being white, I was never fully convinced that God was exclusively Caucasian. There were too many races and cultures and exciting colorations for me to accept the fact that God could be limited to one particular shade. But the original story of creation etched in my impressionable mind persisted in consciousness. It persists today. I still see a vast and whirling uninhabited world and, on the most peaceful and beautiful spot that I can imagine, I see God "coming down" and looking on all that He has made. The sea, the sand, the trees, the land, the rocks and rills, the flora and the fauna and the hills; the fish, the birds, and all the other things that have no words—He looks at them and calls them good. Then God bends down and with His own hands scoops up the dust of the earth. With the touch of a thousand Michelangelos He molds a man, a man substantially more real than any sculptured figure and into it He breathes the breath of life.

At a sentimental level I often feel I was that man. I was he who came to life, whose eyes opened at the sound of God's voice, who caught an instantaneous vision of my Maker, feeling His life as my life, His strength animating me, His thoughts my thoughts, and His spirit mine.

Put up against the hard facts of life, I realize that this literalization of the origin of man bears within it the dynamic essence of all portentous myths. Rich in meaning, it carries my consciousness to another level. I know that something happened to me after that creation experience. God put me into a garden and gave me dominion over all that He had made. He left me in possession of His kingdom, but something went wrong. I couldn't quite work it out, and I have an unforgettable remembrance of glancing back over my shoulder with a longing look at the promised land.

Some interpreters, that is to say philosophers, theologians, and psychoanalysts, claim they know what happened. They call it an apostasy, a fall, inborn sin, temptation, perversion, sex, and the libido. Poets and dramatists also hazard calculated guesses, but I suppose each one of us, deep down in his heart, knows best what actually happened, even though it no longer sounds contemporary: God hid His divinity in us as life itself, and we failed to comprehend or live the greatness of it.

That is one way of looking at things. That is one way of saying that we are prodigals and pilgrims seeking to return to "our Father's house" via all sorts of complicated theological and philosophical paths. Is it true? It seems true. Is it a plausible explanation? It feels that way. Is it the story of man? Many an orthodox Christian will tell you there is no doubt about it.

But one day I was with a group of staff men of the National Geographic Society in Washington, D.C. The subject of conversation was a story about to be run in the *Geographic* (February 1965) having to do with a new find by anthropologists Louis and Mary Leakey. This famous research team had recently discovered the remains of a "Tanganyika man" proved by carbon analysis to have lived and walked upright on the earth 1,820,000 years ago, antedating my preacher uncle's estimate of man's appearance by over 1,800,000 years.

Here we were, comfortably seated in the Madison Hotel in our nation's capital, taking it for granted that we who were enjoying the prime rib and eating properly with shimmering silverware had been in the process of evolution ever since this Tanganyika *homme habilis* (man of ability) built his habitat and ate with his fingers in the African wastelands. Dr. Leakey had given his find the easygoing name of Handyman and when I heard that nickname I felt a real sense of identification. Something told me that I had come up slowly as an evolving phenomenon, had lived through the various and varied stages of genetic and biological change. God had made me, but not full-blown, and because my unfolding had been long and arduous I felt a special nearness to all nature and life in all times and on all levels of experience. I was a handyman and with the ancient poet Rumi I was ready to say,

> "I died as mineral and became a plant,
> I died as plant and rose to animal,
> I died as animal and I was Man.

Why should I fear? When was I ever less by dying?
Yet once more I shall die as Man, to dwell
With angels blest; but even from angelhood
I must travel on."

But then, turning the mirror of reflection upon myself, it suddenly dawned on me that while the origin of mankind was important and while it may have been necessary for me to know where I came from in order to know where I am going, the fact of the matter was that I was here now, here in this particular period in space and time, and there was a life to be lived, a phenomenal life. No matter how I came into being, whether by way of an instant creation or through some endlessly unfolding process—or both—I felt beyond the shadow of doubt that the Creator's life was mine and that I was by nature spiritual.

Finding one's true place in life

Either way, an inner spirit was active in my life and growth. There was a consciousness in me and in every other individual which insisted on expanding, increasing, unfolding. It struggled against difficulties, then converted these difficulties into blessings. It turned defeat into success, apparent failure into triumph, weakness into strength, and through the mysterious alchemy of faith had the power to change darkness into light.

I had often seen this consciousness at work. I saw it in Albert Schweitzer in Lambarene where it caused a man of genius and talent to invest his life in unusual social service. I had observed it in Vinoba Bhave in India, a wisp of a man who became a symbol for stewardship and selfless effort through his Bhoodan movement. I had seen the phenomenon personified in Dr. Larry Mellon in the Haitian jungle where he founded a hospital to serve the needs of those less fortunately born than he. I had discovered it in Tenko Nishida in Japan whose settlement at Yamashina became a symbol of changed and dedicated lives. Seemingly everywhere I found friends and acquaintances whose names, though they never made news, had at a deep level of feeling found their true place in life.

They discovered consciousness, as Emerson once said, to be "a sliding scale with life above life in infinite degrees."

"As I wander through the dark," Helen Keller reported, "I am aware of encouraging voices that murmur from the spirit realm. I sense a holy passion pouring from the springs of Infinity. I thrill to music that beats with the pulse of God. Bound to suns and planets by invisible cords, I feel the flame of eternity in my soul."

Every life of consciousness has to be a free life, accepting reality at whatever level and in whatever situation it finds itself, trying always to interpret things from the highest possible point of view. Consciousness is the indwelling spirit of true life, representing the power to become, changing and remaking lives everywhere, every day, among those willing to feel and explore the commonly unfelt.

This was where I had to take my stand. Where was I to look for meaning if not within myself? Whom was I to trust if not the presence of creative life in me? What was I to express if not the evidence of something deeply felt? Looking into the mirror of reflection I knew that the eyes with which I "saw God" were truly His eyes seeing me. Anything less than this was an escape from my true awareness and a degradation of my innermost belief.

A report from Tanganyika or the dogmatic view of a preacher uncle, what did it matter? The truth, I told myself, is that I am here *now* and there is a life to be lived, an exciting, adventurous life which asks at every stage of joy or distress, through every experience of triumph or loss, healing or hurt, "You have told me how your body feels. How do *you* feel?"

Always there is consciousness, beguiling us with the inescapable question, "What are you doing about the phenomenon of you?"

XI ✱ EXPECTATION

When I think of the unscientific, homespun upbringing I had, I marvel that I turned out as well as I did. No Dr. Spock, no Montessori school, no psychological guidance, no character measurements, no Rorschach test; none of these figured in my coming of age, not even a Roentgen kymograph which charts the art of sucking, swallowing, and breathing. Yet I never got into any serious scrapes, was never hauled before a judge or jury, never, so far as I know, disgraced my parents or myself overly much. On the contrary, as long as I am singing these *a cappella* praises, let me mention that I was Exhibit A when it came to filling a niche worthy of our family hall of fame, such as it is.

I was twelve when, after I had done exceptionally well in a music competition, my mother complimented me and added, "I am especially proud of you because you were one child I really didn't want."

Such an admission nowadays would send both mother and child into nine months of analytical sessions and possibly a series of shock treatments. I considered my mater's statement an exciting compliment. Here I was, uninvited but making good! Here I stood, an accident of birth, but apparently in divine order! It was wonderful. I remember how my mother laughed and embraced me and how I felt uniquely special whenever I reflected that I was an unwanted wanted child.

I often think of this when I am counseling with students. Some tell me with great concern that they were adopted and hadn't been advised of it or that they learned they were illegitimate or that they have feelings of unwantedness. Others complain there is a gap between their parents and themselves, that their dads don't understand them, they don't understand their dads, there's a gulf they can't bridge, they can't communicate; and constantly there is the commonplace complaint that, "I don't know what to do with my life and there is no one at home to counsel me."

I try to remember whether my dad ever counseled me, and I can't. I cannot recall a time that my father and I ever sat down for a man-to-man talk. The facts of life were never discussed. Sex was never mentioned. I would be hard put to explain where I learned what I learned about what every young man should know. As for a career, I was on my own with no parental strings attached. In everything, with the possible exception of religion, I was a free traveler on an open road. But I was lucky. My father impressed just one indelible phrase on me, words that stuck like a brand mark on a maverick. He simply said, "All I expect of you, my boy, is that you do something worth-while with your life."

My mother, who by no means agreed with everything my father said and who never actually counseled me with any long-range view, did concur in this paternal directive, "All we expect of you is that you do something worth-while with your life."

Whether it was the way it was said or the calculated timing when it was said, or if there was a certain receptivity on my part while it was said, I have never figured out. I only know that an expectation was born in me and that it sensitized me to life, has kept me sensitized, and serves, as far as I know, as a solid basis for feeling the commonly unfelt. I am disposed by nature to great expectations. Even the Scripture saying, "To whom much has been given, much is expected," has affected my disposition. Much was given to me, not in the way of counsel and advice and admonitions, but in the way of camaraderie. But even that was never overly intimate. It was comfortable, a comfortable feeling challenging me with a goal: it was expected that I do something worth-while with my life.

There were certain unwritten precepts in our household which were rarely discussed and only infrequently broken. Everyone simply expected everyone in the household to abide by them. For instance, there was the wine decanter. This lovely crystal piece with its rose-colored contents was a natural fixture on the dining-room buffet. None of us four children ever thought about taking a sip out of it, though I cannot remember that we were ever warned not to. So, too, my father regularly enjoyed his Thursday nights in the town tavern over a game of German *Skat*. My mother frowned on this, especially since the local priest was one of the players. She was more afraid of Catholic contamination than she was of Schlitz. Yet none of us boys ever gave cards or beer or the tavern a serious thought. We were expected to know that things acceptable for Dad might not be good for us. Nor were we surprised when later on in life my father gave up *Skat* and my mother began to fraternize with the Catholics. There was nothing righteous about it either way.

Fishing with father

I remember during the deep-feeling years of my boyhood, I went fishing with my father one Sunday morning despite the objections of my church-devoted mother. Most youngsters today would take such an outing as a lark, but for me it was a fateful decision.

Sunday morning was structured on the expectation that everyone would unquestioningly go to Sunday school and church. But on this particular Sabbath the fishing season was scheduled to open at the crack of dawn. Now actually my father was a fairly dedicated churchman, but after a hard week at the store the Sunday out-of-doors called a good deal louder and more appealingly than the old church bell, especially when the Wisconsin earth was breaking forth with spring.

My mother contended we could go fishing before the service or afterward, though that would be sinful enough, but my father, a well-versed Waltonian, explained that by some divine quirk the crappies bit best from ten to twelve, exactly the hours for Sunday School and church.

Why my mother did not say, "Well, you go but leave the boy here," I will never know, unless there was a strange kind of unspoken love and wisdom behind it all. At any rate, it meant that she would have to face *Herr Pastor* as well as the horror of several aunts who already had me slated for the ministry at the age of ten.

So we took the devil by the horns and pedaled our bikes the four miles to Lodi's Mill, where a willow-sheltered pond provided a popular crappie and sunfish habitat. Cane poles strapped to our bicycles betrayed to churchgoing cars where we were headed. Minnow bait in canvas buckets strapped to our handlebars, sandwiches and pop in our bike baskets, we skimmed over the blacktopped highway with a song in our hearts, and not necessarily a church song either.

Great expectations.

Great expectations made me want to do things well whether riding the bike or thinking great thoughts, and every detail of that Sunday adventure stands out brave and clear, actually more clear than brave because the road to Lodi's Mill near Sauk City, where we lived, led past the town cemetery, and as I glimpsed the jagged rows of headstones my thoughts were anything but courageous. My uncle's preachments had impressed upon me the fact that these gruesome, weather-scarred markers were God's trump card. We might escape His wrath, even as we were escaping the morning services, but He would get us in the end. It did not matter whether a person was Protestant or Catholic, or whether the cemeteries were strictly segregated between the two faiths as they were in my hometown: man's mortal end was there for all to see, no matter which of the iron gates the coal-black hearse drove through.

But suddenly a sense of victory surged through me. I was with my father. We were side by side on man-sized bikes, riding together as if we had found a knowledge bigger than death and dying. A flash of secret wisdom told me I knew things that even my preacher uncle did not know, knew them because I felt them on this beautiful spring morning. God liked fishing. Jesus liked fishermen. God liked this Sunday-morning world. He liked the green and growing pine trees better than He did the stained old marble stones. The mounds of tended grass, the lifeless slabs, the rusted iron crosses in these weeping acres were not the true world at all. "Don't let them fool you!" an inner voice was saying to me. "Don't let these man-made markers which the workmen have set in hard concrete so that they can't be pushed over on Halloween get mixed up with God. Consider the trees and the sumac! And what do you see when you look at the roses making beautiful the cemetery's white picket fence?"

God's world was life and freedom. God's world was the open road and the farmyards and the young corn coming up in clean cultivated fields. God's world was the man-sized bike and the legs that made the wheels go round. God's world was Dad and I and Lodi's Mill. God's world included people going to church or going fishing, just as long as they really loved the Lord.

In the all-encompassing bigness of that world I saw my mother, too, as part of God's great and wonderful plan. I saw her dressed in her Sunday finest, hat properly on her head, white gloves drawn up to her elbows, her patent-leather purse dangling from her arm, her Peloubet Sunday-school notes folded neatly into her white Bible. God's world. It was big enough to take in Uncle *Pfarrer* with his black *mütze* and his stern, unsmiling face, and his long black pulpit coat, the tail of which once got caught in the pulpit door. Thank you, God, for your sense of humor! And thank you for the silent beauty of Lodi's Mill where we laid our bikes in the deep grass and stalked our way silently to the water's unruffled edge.

Great expectations. The green flakes of algae covering the breathless pond, the shimmering lily pads, the beds of watercress, the silent mill, the green carpeted hills, the sound of frogs, the sight of unhurried clouds, the motionless figures of other fishermen, the scent of willows brought a church song singing in my mind:

"Come Thou Almighty King,
Help us Thy Name to sing,
Help us to praise,
Father all Glorious.
O'er all victorious,
Come and reign over us,
Ancient of days."

Church time. But now the ritual was my father casting bait and bobber into a strategic clearing among the reeds and lilies. I, a willing acolyte, tried to do as well. Then we waited, prayerful and expectant, until a bobber disappeared with a smack, scattering the algae and ripping a lily pad from its muddy moorings. Then came a Sabbath-breaking splash and in a moment my dad was stringing a glistening crappie on a willow bough.

Church time and the fish were fighting hungry. Soon we were stringing our catch according to size while carefully disengaging the smaller frys and letting them go. It was a perfect morning and, for some untold reason, I felt no sense of guilt in the midst of blessing, only an overpowering feeling of love and understanding for my preacher uncle and for all my other relatives who were keeping the church fires burning.

I matured that morning more than I had in many a year. It dawned on me that there is something a person wants more than happiness for himself and something he wishes for more than even a mess of fish: an awareness of God's good and God's approachableness, an expectation of rightness and freedom in His presence, and a sensitive response to all life everywhere.

Nowadays I talk of fishing for marlin at Mazatlán and of the salmon run in the Frazer. I sing the praises of steelheads and the kokanee which I have sought in many waters, but memory carries no deeper feeling than the Sunday morning at Lodi's Mill. A sensitivity was born that day, and it was signed and sealed when my father and I came home and proudly dumped our colorful catch into the kitchen sink.

"Well," said my mother with an exaggerated sigh of marvel and concern, "what is a person to say?"

"Say it was good fishing," said my father.

"But on a Sunday," my mother lamented, "and during church time at that."

With a wink at me my father remarked, "We have enough to take a mess to *Onkel Pfarrer*."

My mother threw up her hands. "I should say not!" she exclaimed. "It is better for everyone to think you didn't catch any at all."

But she was already tying on her apron and calling for the fish knife as if the mill pond, for just a moment in the rush of time, might have been the Sea of Galilee.

A miracle we can all perform

I am disposed by nature to great expectations. I believe in them, anticipate them, invite them, and therefore usually find them verified in the experience of others who, as I, bring them to life by first feeling them *in* life.

I thought of this recently in Toronto, Canada, when I visited Avery Cooke, who was observing his centennial birthday. There he was, walking like a man of sixty, enthusiastically showing a group of visitors his rose garden. I asked him the inevitable question, "To what do you attribute your long life and your wonderful health?"

"Well, I'll tell you," he said, "I just never expected anything else. I expected I'd live to see a hundred. I expected to be well. I expected to be just what I am, so there is no miracle about it at all."

No miracle excepting the miracle of great expectations, a miracle that we can all perform if we put our minds to it. Expectation is a feeling. It generates the qualities needed for the attainment of the goal, qualities that get into the subconscious and chart a pattern. Theoreticians say, "Think great, visualize greatness, hope greatly, and be grateful." My father said, "All I expect of you is that you do something worth-while with your life."

He had enough of an assignment doing something with his life, and that may be why he turned me over to myself. He let it be known that the one person whom I could do something with was *me*. I could best take up the challenge of my life. I could most clearly see the unseen within myself and hear the unheard and feel the commonly unfelt. I and I alone could expect some hint of divinity in my life and try to live up to it. Only I could keep turning back the layers of doubt and guilt, the masks and the make-believe, the aims and aspirations until I came down to the real *me*, and there would always be moments in which I would be called upon to prove the person I professed and hoped to be.

It was said that when the ship *Lakonia* went down near the Madeiras there was a man among the lifeboat survivors dressed in a neat suit, a tweed topcoat over his arm, and carrying a brief-case. He refused help when he climbed aboard the rescue ship *Salta* and calmly aided other survivors as they came aboard. An officer on the *Salta* congratulated him on his composure and asked for an explanation. The man replied, "I'm an Englishman, sir. It is expected of me."

The stuff wishes are made of

Expectation is a servant of the will, the will is the result of a wish, and a wish is spun from the power of spirit. This is far from explaining the entire nature of it, nor does it answer the question why some individuals seem more spiritually or psychically motivated than others. Some people do respond more readily to a deep-feeling level, perhaps because they sense the reward of it, desire the joy of it, feel the challenge of it, or anticipate the karmic good of it.

Some say, "I expect nothing out of life one way or the other." Yet even that is quite an expectation! It is like the Oriental who says, "I desire only desirelessness." Expectation presupposes faith. It is faith plus, faith felt, faith fortified.

Even when expectation is hidden behind a negativism, it makes things happen. Had I not been introduced to Iowa farmers I might never have understood this, but during my years in the Midwest I got to know them and admire them. They are a special breed. They will never let you see their deeper selves. They hide their emotions. They shy away from admitting their true love for nature or the land. After you have lived with them for any length of time, you will want to revise your whole concept of the power of positive thinking, for they are as negative about success as a fox would have you believe it is negative about chickens.

Spring, according to the farmers' customary complaint, comes too early or too late. The ground at planting time is too wet or too dry. The corn grows too slow or too fast. The market is too unsteady or too fixed. Harvest time comes too soon or not soon enough. Yet rarely, if ever, does the Iowa farmer fail to have a bumper crop and never in my extended sojourn in the Hawkeye State did he ever have a bad year. On the contrary, heaven opens its windows on him as if he had a magic combination. He now produces 175 bushels of corn per acre where once he got less than ninety. He will never let you in on it, but he is playing a game, a game of great expectations behind a make-believe of discontent through which, if you look closely, you will see him smile. He doesn't even want nature or the land to know how great his faith in their ability actually is. Don't say it, he warns, think it. Don't talk about it, feel it.

Mask your expectations. Do not let even the fates catch on to the greatness and depths of your desires. How deeply did my father's expectation for me actually go? How great was his concern, how strong was his wish? Wisely, shrewdly, he never let me know. He sowed the seed just deeply enough at just the right time and evidently he knew the nature of the planting.

I have great expectations for getting good mail. Sometimes this gets to be a phobia. I get good letters, life-changing letters because I expect them, but if I ever dropped my game of make-believe that mail doesn't really matter, I would lose my magic touch.

It is a subtle and, at times, a difficult game. Take, for example, the old adage that "expectation is greater than realization." This is generally true and we ought by rights hold it as a basic truth at a deep level of feeling. Failing to do this, we must keep relearning the same lesson over and over again. Expect greatly, but expect, too, that expectation is usually greater than realization.

The art of planning

It is an extremely fine art, this matter of planning without planning too hard, of visualizing without creating a rigid dream, of programming without setting up such a tight agenda that the spirit of spontaneity has no room in which to move. All of which eventually brings one around to the conclusion that life taken in stride is fully as rich and rewarding as life planned by design.

Recently we invited a friend up to our guest house, *The Crow's Nest*, tucked away on a wooded hill with a wonderful view of lake and mountains and with a feeling of quietude so rare that a robin immediately appropriated one of the logs below the overhang and confidently hatched out its chirping brood. My wife and I were excited about the prospect of having everything shipshape for our first guest, a bachelor friend of long standing who, we were sure, was precisely the one to initiate and bless this house.

We thought we knew his likes and dislikes—no noise, a shelf of good books, colorful draperies, good lighting, no guests, plenty of hot water, and so on. We fell more and more in love with *The Crow's Nest* as we readied it with great expectations.

Like Nicodemus, our friend came at night, which, I have now discovered, is the worst possible time for a guest to come straight from a bustling city to a mountain retreat. The contrast is too great, the night too awesome, the silence too deep, even though a hi-fi is calming the air with subdued welcoming music.

The lake, lovely in the daytime or when the moon is bright, lay ink black and eerie along the shadowy shore line, making strange murmuring sighs as the restless water lapped against the lonely crags. We thought *The Crow's Nest* looked intriguing with its mellow lights and soft décor, but I felt our guest's vibrations when I told him he would be "absolutely alone," and that the soft whisper of the wind would "lull him to sleep." All of which apparently was the very worst welcome we could possibly have accorded him. He was not used to being absolutely alone. He did not want the wind to lull him to sleep. I realized this when he asked pointed questions about the locks on the doors and about the distance from the guest house to the main cabin. I knew when he spotted a diffident spider in the bathtub that he was unused to the Canadian out-of-doors and, when he asked with a start, "What's that?" as the mother robin took a night flight past the window screen, I knew that our high hope for a housewarming was growing cold.

At six in the morning there was a banging at our cabin door. My friend stood there, haggard and abashed, oblivious of the beauty of sunrise over the lake and deaf to the entrancing warble of a loon out on the open waters.

"Dammit!" he said. "I had a miserable night!"

Over a pot of coffee he recounted his complaints, the list of which caused me to hang my head in shame. The new hot-water heater had gurgled and regurgitated all night long, setting up banshee sounds that curdled his blood. The toilet stuck and he had to remove the top and adjust the plunger, always a messy job. There were peculiar tappings on the roof—I had neglected to tell him that a tree squirrel occasionally used it as a short cut from tree to tree. The lock on the door didn't lock, and another spider had crawled up through the bathtub drain. Moaning with exhaustion, he wondered if he might flop down in the big cabin and get some rest, which is what he did, and which was what he might have done from the start had we not had such high expectations that *The Crow's Nest* was outfitted exactly for him. He stayed only two days and the robins never even got to know his name.

Then I think of the unexpected, unprepared, unannounced visitors who have come down the lane and who, even though we sometimes shuddered to think how their visit would pan out, brought the informal warmth and joy that only spontaneity can bring. No preparations were made, no rooms were cleaned in advance, no program was worked out, no illusions were built up one way or another. Everything turned out to be in order because we had not had time to tamper with destiny's plans.

Evidently there is a divine current of some kind ready to carry us through certain phases of life, and the more we realize this and give ourselves over to it, the better off we are. Yet who has the courage to believe it, the daring to expect it, the wisdom to understand it, or the prudence to conform to it?

A reluctant swimmer who has come close to drowning can hardly be impressed with the confident assurance that "the water is your friend!" Even drownproofing seems to him merely an insidious technique to help him drown all the faster. Sometimes, though, it is possible by an act of grace or by some recognition of the deeper self to get the feeling of the friendliness for the mystic stream. For it is a feeling, the art of feeling the commonly unfelt.

Truly successful people always hold great expectations even though, like the Iowa farmer, they may hedge a bit. Brave men, though fearful, are never afraid of fear. Healthy persons have no time for sickness, and to the pure of heart things are not as impure as they seem.

We catch on to the truth and technique of expectation in those rare moments when we are stirred by an awareness of a guidance seemingly higher and greater than our own, when for a little while we are taken over by a force and an intelligence above and beyond those commonly felt. Confident and free, filled with wonder and ready acceptance, we permit ourselves to be taken over by our unquestioning self. How can we repeat these experiences? One way is to expect their repetition and to feel ourselves worthy of having them happen again.

Reasons for failure

My father tried to impress it upon me that people patronized the business places that gave evidence of affluence and success. I disagreed. I wanted to trade at the places which were having a hard time of it. I felt for them. But gradually I learned that my feeling was misplaced and that in identifying myself with them I was thinking failure instead of success and that my attitude was more patronizing than sincere. I also eventually tired of their complaining, their contention that they were not getting the breaks, that people were against them, and that they were probably born under an unlucky star. But there are reasons for failure and success beyond the zodiac, and the art of expectation on the proper level is the key.

There is a significant saying in the Book of Job, "The thing that I have feared has come upon me," and I have seen the truth of this demonstrated many times. Among a group of travelers whom I took to the Orient was a man who complained bitterly when the stewardess neglected to serve him his coffee. "She passed me by," he reported. "She served everyone around me and left me sitting here. But that always happens to me. I fully expect it." Sure enough, on the return flight with an entirely new crew, the stewardess not only forgot to bring his coffee, she forgot to serve him his meal. Fiery mad, he pressed the call button. "I'm so sorry," said the stewardess. "I can't imagine how I overlooked you." "They all do it to me!" he told her. They all did. And Job was right.

While house-hunting in southern California we were shown a place which a woman was renting temporarily. She said, "I wanted to buy a place in a certain section in Santa Barbara but was told there wasn't adequate fire protection. I live in deathly fear of fires. So I didn't buy. I came down to L.A. and bought a house in a canyon. Two months after I moved in I was burned out. You know, I think I carried that fire with me."

Wise old Job. But what did Job do about it? What can anyone do about it when he expects the worst and by his expectation invites the worst to happen?

We can do what Job did. We can learn that if we have a propensity for fear, we have an even greater propensity for faith. If we think we are slated for failure, it may be because we know we are meant for success. Our negative expectations are our positive determinations gone astray, but they are not *gone*. We come back to the formula: expectation is a matter of feeling, feeling is a servant of the will, the will is the result of a wish, and a wish is spun from the power of spirit.

Just how this works, or by what kind of a psychological test this can be measured, I do not know. My father never told me. In fact, the only thing he ever said was, "All I expect of you is that you do something worth-while with your life."

XII * APPREHENSION

There are many ways to get to the Holy Land. You can go by land, sea, or air. Some devotees insist on walking and one intrepid pilgrim from Old Mexico made it on a burro. Several people have told me they have gone there "in spirit" without ever leaving their homes and symbolically they may have been quite right. As for me, I went by plane, but must agree with my fellow passengers that we were borne on angels' wings.

Storms are nothing new to airline crews and weather hazards are generally routine, but to the Christian traveler who is bound to have all sorts of sentiments, hopes, and superstitions about this sainted land, two hours in turbulence over old Jerusalem can be a sampling of the final judgment.

I have an innate fatalism about flying. Like most people who depend on the airlines almost exclusively, I have the unquestioned belief that the plane will always deliver me safely to my destination, even if an engine conks out. At this particular point there is no doubt whatsoever in my mind and no two ways about it. I would never think of betraying this confidence in air travel by taking out flight insurance. On the other hand, on another level of feeling, I cannot for the life of me imagine how these thousands of daily flights in all parts of the world, with their infinite margins for human error and an equal margin for mechanical and meteorological hazards, can continue to maintain their fantastic record of safety; yet they do despite anyone's apprehension.

But to come to the Holy Land.

I had boarded the Viscount at Beirut and the seat-belt sign had been on continuously. It was rough-and-ready flying. The thunderheads through which we knifed our way were like gutted walls waiting further demolition. The sky itself resembled a bombed-out city as we threaded through the cloud debris. The storm had already stretched the customary sixty-minute flight into two grueling hours.

The *No Smoking* warning had been flashed on over the Jerusalem airport some thirty minutes before, simultaneously with the stewardess's calm announcement that we were preparing to put down. She revised this moments later with the advice that the rain and wind would temporarily delay our landing. She did not mention the lightning.

Lightning is a powerful leveler actually and figuratively. A Viscount bottled up in a storm is an exciting envoy into the unknown. Between the two, the effect is sobering.

We had made one attempt to land in a grim gray swirl of rain and mist shortly before dusk. Caught in a powerful crosswind and bombarded by the tempest, the plane swooped upward with a scream of combat.

The clatter of the rain on the wings so close to the runway had nonetheless been a welcome, reassuring sound. For a moment, at least, we had felt a nearness to Mother Earth and as we zoomed upward I had a strange and haunted feeling that we were leaving her for a long, long time.

Around a bend a fellow goes. . . .

Once more above the rain our circling pattern continued monotonously, endlessly, sometimes, it seemed to me, hopelessly. I resigned myself, as one always does, to the skill of the crew and the airworthiness of the craft. I relaxed and in a moment of reflection there came to mind an evening at home when, as a college student, I had returned for the Easter holidays. It was Holy Week and on a rainy spring night my parents and I sat in the warm fireplace comfort of our open-beamed living room. The remembrance of the rain on the roof that night had very likely been awakened by the rain I had heard on the plane. At any rate, the events of that evening returned vividly and nostalgically.

My mother loved to recite poetry, a penchant which involves the same hazards as home movies. When the program gets going, there is no way of finding an appropriate close. My mother was proud of having memorized great cantos of Goethe and Schiller, to say nothing of a liberal seasoning of Robert Frost. For lyrical fare her loves were James Weldon Johnson and Thomas Moore.

On this particular night she was preparing a program for a church function and drew out of her phenomenal repertory Moore's *O Think Not My Spirits*. When she came to the lines, "And the heart that is soonest awake to the flowers, is always the first to be touched by the thorn," my father said, "Now what do you suppose that means?"

Miffed at his interruption my mother exclaimed, "Must everything have a meaning? Can't you just *feel* it?"

"I could feel it more if I knew what it meant," he replied.

"It's poetry," my mother protested. But then, as if contemplating what she would say if someone in her audience would ask my father's question, she repeated the words thoughtfully, "And the heart that is soonest awake to the flowers, is always the first to be touched by the thorn."

My father drew eloquently at his cigar as if an inscrutable idea were emerging out of the twirling smoke.

"I was just thinking," he submitted, "that it ought to be the other way around. A person who really appreciates a flower shouldn't mind the thorns."

"It's poetry," my mother repeated with make-believe exasperation. "You don't have to read all sorts of things into it. Just enjoy it."

I laughed to myself at the clarity of this recall. Why did this remembrance return to me up here in the darkening clouds above Jerusalem? How was I to explain the sensation that the curved shield of the plane had momentarily become a beamed ceiling and that the ship's cramped surroundings were actually a cozy retreat in a big frame house in the Wisconsin hills? How does the mind or the feeling factor select one particular setting out of the endless reels of well-remembered scenes? The plane pitched and convulsed in the swash of wind, sharp flashes of lightning opened devouring jaws and snapped at us as we prowled through walls of cloud and mist, but it was more real to me that I was seated in the living room of my parental home.

"Roses and thorns," my father was saying, leveling a puff of smoke toward the ceiling. "I was thinking that if you want a poem about flowers, why don't you use the one that says, 'Around a bend a fellow goes, and right ahead he sees a rose.' Remember that?"

"Remember that!" I heard my mother say in fraudulent disgust. "That's not from Moore anyway, that's from Douglas Malloch."

And though I never thought I knew these particular lines, it was as if I heard them loud and clear:

"Along the journey here and there
You often find a flower,
Just anytime or anywhere,
No special place or hour.
They are not planted in a row;
You never guess, you never know;
Around a bend a fellow goes,
And right ahead he sees a rose."

The words seemed almost as if they were coming over the speaker system in the plane, and the scene persisted as if projected on a screen in full range for me to see. I could hear the rain on the shingled roof and feel the friendly warmth of the open hearth.

Seldom did my mother show any extreme emotion or openly betray her feelings, but I recalled how she stood behind my father's chair and gently put her hands on his shoulders. "Why did you wonder if I remembered that?" she asked. "You know it was one of the first poems I learned from the book you gave me, *The Heart Content.*"

"At least it does away with the thorns," said my father, covering her hands with his. "I was thinking that a person can take his choice about almost everything whether it's poetry or just plain living. You can lean either way, to what's good or what's bad. That's up to each one of us."

I remembered something else about that night, something that now returned through the fury of the storm and the incessant whine of the plane: there is no greater art in life than to feel the commonly unfelt and keep the feeling to oneself. Though I had never become proficient in this department, I knew the reach and power of it, for the art of *this* kind of apprehension is of a special kind and is always present in people you never forget; the depth of feeling is there, felt but not revealed, present but not on exhibition, a soul stuff tucked away in life's sacred corner, in a hidden place around the bend. And perhaps those who live this way, those "whose hearts are soonest awake to the flowers," cannot help being the first to be touched by the thorn.

Flying in a storm

In classical language, apprehension can be the anticipation of unfavorable happenings or it can be, as philosophers insist, the cognition of the absolute essence of things. It is a conscious knowing beyond reason and judgment, truly an affair of the heart.

An announcement in Arabic came through the crackling static of the speaker system. I waited for the translation. "We are still over Jerusalem," the pilot reported. "We will try for a landing in a little while. The stewardess will give you instructions. Thank you."

I glanced around at the passengers, for I had only briefly noticed them when I hurried aboard at Beirut. Now I felt a kinship with them. We had something in common: apprehension in the customary sense. Uneasiness was making itself felt. Concern became a thing of feeling. A bid for solidarity was initiated by the very nature of our nearness to things unknown.

The story of *The Bridge of San Luis Rey* flashed through my mind. On that occasion destiny brought a group of travelers together on a fateful summer's day, brought them together from various walks of life at the exact time and place on a Peruvian bridge when the structure mysteriously collapsed. Why, asked author

Thornton Wilder, were these five people in this specific location at this specific time? Why were they and they alone flung to death in the gorge below? The question had so intrigued a Franciscan, Brother Juniper by name, that he assigned himself the task of tracing the lives of the victims backward into time in order to find an answer for their common fate. "Brother Juniper," Wilder reported, "thought he saw in this accident the wicked visited by destruction and the good called early to heaven."

Who, I wondered, has not done serious thinking along these lines and who has not concluded that an invisible world stretches out from this visible world of ours on either side? Are we not all riding on wings of the unknown? Are we not all crossing bridges? Do we not all have a hunch that our brief earth life is but a small arc in the total circumference of the life of the soul?

I had the confident feeling that nothing could possibly happen to us in the Viscount. I knew that everything would turn out safely and yet I would not have been surprised if it had turned out otherwise. Did the wayfarers on the bridge of San Luis Rey have a premonition that theirs was to be their last crossing? Were they conscious of the fact that the Keeper of Dreams had His own dream and plan in mind? Do we by our own doing bring ourselves to our own point of destiny? Was it inevitable that we in the plane, thirty-three of us, should be together, each having been called from his own remote and secret corner of existence? As the Viscount sang its solemn requiem to the angry clouds, my questioning thoughts took on a sequence: San Luis Rey—flowers and thorns—around a bend a fellow goes——

Across the aisle from me sat a swarthy, middle-aged Moslem. His strong brown hands were wrapped around by a string of large amber beads, his "rosary." These he clasped and unclasped, twisted, fingered, and counted them over and over again. Next to him on the window side sat his wife in purdah. This white garment covered her completely from head to toe, concealing her face and figure as thoroughly as if she were in a tent, with one exception. The purdah had a tiny peephole of gauze across the hooded covering of the face. No more than six inches broad and an inch wide, this allowed her to squint at the world around. I wondered why she sat near the window, for surely she must have had difficulty glimpsing even the livid streams of lightning that poured past the plane.

Most of all I wondered what these two followers of Islam were thinking? He with his worry beads and disconsolate face; she inside her impenetrable shroud. What kind of thoughts, what kind of feeling, what sort of questioning went on in their minds? Or were they merely saying trustfully to themselves, "It is the will of Allah!" Whatever comes, the will of Allah.

Directly in front of me a young Jordanian in uniform kept pushing himself back restlessly in his chair until I braced my knees against his shoving. Earlier, before we encountered the full force of the storm, this black-haired fellow had been chain smoking. When the "No Smoking" sign flashed on, he had to be warned by the purser to put out his cigarette. From then on he began squirming in his seat.

Across from him sat an elderly dark-complexioned woman wearing black gloves and a disheveled mantilla. Her black Persian lamb coat served as a blanket covering her legs and tucked into her seat belt. Murmuring to herself what sounded like an Italian prayer of self-pity, she had the stewardess at her beck and call, apparently never realizing that the girl had to reach her side by clinging to each swaying seat on the lurching plane. At the moment she was accepting from the stewardess several pills and attempting to take a sip of water out of a partially filled cup.

In answer to her lament the stewardess said in a voice loud enough for others to hear, "You can trust the pilot."

Behind me a baby cried. A young American with her child in arms had been on the flight with me from Rome and had also just made connections with the Viscount. Across from her a red-faced, red-haired man slumped in his seat fast asleep. His brightly flowered tie was loosed, his white shirt open, and his sagging body tugged at the seat belt with every roll of the plane. Further back, a woman traveler obviously airsick was excitedly calling for the purser who hurried to her side.

The stubborn moan of the engines carried on their droning dialogue with the arguing wind. I could not rid myself of the feeling that we who sat here in the plane had something to do with the weather. Of course we didn't, but still I felt we did. We helped to make things happen, not entirely perhaps, but to a greater degree than we cared to admit. I had a hunch that everyone in the Viscount knew this and believed it. We were players in a drama that we had written. A collaboration, sponsored by the fact that we had been brought together into this lonely, ominous flight. We had written the script aided by the mysterious co-author God, writing much or little according to our conjecture and His will.

Suddenly the plane was picked up and shaken by an especially strong arm of the storm which held it for a moment and then abruptly let it go, depositing the stewardess into the vacant seat next to me.

"Doing all right?" she asked with a laugh, reaching for the seat belt.

"I *heard* that the Holy Land was a trouble spot," I said.

"I have seen it as bad in Copenhagen," she murmured. "That is home for me."

The purser was making his way to the side of the woman with the mantilla who was moaning in distress. The stewardess started to get up, but he motioned her to remain where she was while he sat down next to the woman and quieted her. In front of me the young Jordanian pushed and shoved. Across the aisle the Moslem counted his beads while his ghostlike wife sat in motionless silence.

"You mind it?" asked the stewardess, indicating the lightning.

"I have been in storms before," I managed to say. "They tell me a plane is a safe place to be when it's lightning. They say the same thing about metal boats. I never believed it, but sometimes in a pinch a person believes what he doesn't believe."

"I know what you mean," she said, turning herself around to check the state of her clientele and to see that all was fairly well under control. "But," she asked with a fling of her head, "what do you think of him?"

"Him?" I followed her glance to a passenger three seats ahead of ours across the aisle, to a man all but hidden from where I sat. In fact, but for the squirming Jordanian who had now tilted his seat almost into my lap, I might not have noticed this traveler even now. But I did notice him and it was quite a shock, for this seemingly unperturbed gentleman was sitting with clipboard in hand writing on a sheaf of yellow sheets with absolute calm.

I say it was a shock, but in a way it was more of a fantasy, for it has always been a practice of mine to carry exactly such a clipboard and always with yellow sheets just as this stranger was doing. On the seat of my car, in planes, on trains, even in boats, I am never without this mood-maker, this handy scratch pad, for I am always writing, always jotting down impressions, even though two thirds of them are never used and usually never looked at again. I do it because of my frugality with ideas. On this trip, however, I had inadvertently put the clipboard into my bag that had been checked through. I had missed it all the way from Rome.

Put it down as a coincidence, but why should a man over Jerusalem be using a clipboard exactly like mine! What are the astronomical chances for something like this to happen and what does ESP have to say about that? Around a bend a fellow goes, and suddenly. . . .

I tried to get a clearer view of the stranger's face, a brown, serene face, sharply featured, a bald head which might at one time have been shaved tonsure fashion. Inquiringly I turned to the stewardess, but she was extricating herself from her seat belt and hurrying away to answer the call of the airsick woman at the rear of the plane.

But for the jostling and pitching of our trustworthy ship and the obvious warning of the seat-belt sign, I would have been bold enough to go over to this traveler and ask him what thoughts he was putting down on his yellow sheets. I watched the dreamy, casual movement of his pencil and noticed that he had moments when, caught by inspiration, he wrote as furiously as if he wished to match the behavior of the storm.

I knew the feeling. There have been times when I felt myself a channel for such *furor scribendi,* wonderful inspired moments when thoughts came thick and fast and my #2 Ticonderoga was unable to keep up with the onrush of ideas. Later, reflective reading warned me that what I had considered great lines were but an illusion, a dream, marvelous in the whirl of inspiration but fearfully inadequate upon "waking." Yet these were good moments nonetheless.

The Hindus call it "darshan"

The Viscount prowled on. The stranger continued to write and when he adjusted himself in his seat he seemed actually to be laughing quietly to himself, as if being a pawn for the storm was part of the prescribed routine of flight. He gave me confidence. In fact, since he had some of the features of an Indian, a Hindu, I said to myself, "He gives me *darshan!*" That was a good word. Darshan means a power and a fortitude that come to a person merely by being in the presence of a great soul. That was why the Hindus flocked in such numbers to see Pope Paul during his India visit. They did not want Catholicism, they wanted *darshan.* That is why they followed Gandhi. They did not care so much for freedom from Great Britain as they did for *darshan.* That is why they were beginning to love the memory of Dr. Schweitzer. They had not agreed with his interpretation of Hinduism, but they knew he had something that rubbed off: *darshan. Darshan* is empathy, consciousness, expectation, apprehension of the highest possible sort, the instinctive knowing that goodness eventually wins over evil, strength over weakness, faith over fear. *Darshan* is hope around the bend. . . .

As I was thinking this, the dark walls of the sky suddenly opened and hurled a ball of light out of the scream of the storm. It was like an impact with a sheet of flame that seemed to dissolve the shield of our ship with a tongue of fire and a rush of wind. The Viscount gave the impression of hanging for an instant stunned and paralyzed, and in the space of that blinding flash we went through an eternity of light and sound.

I came to myself and looked around. There was no sign of panic. No one seemed any the worse for the experience and strangely no one had so much as cried out. Even the woman with the mantilla was less frightened now than she had been before. The Jordanian was quiet. The Moslem looked down at his beads while his hooded wife turned her face toward the window. The red-faced man, roused from his sluggish slumber, yawned and shook the sleep from his eyes. When I turned to look at the other passengers, I noticed the young mother calmly lulling her child. As for the man with the clipboard, he sat, as before, writing, as if the lightning which had struck the plane and rolled off into space had been nothing more than a sudden flash of inspiration or the afterglow of a great idea.

There was an announcement in Arabic over the speaker system. The pilot, with an obvious edge of relief in his voice, said, "Really sorry about that one. Now that it has it out of its system we are being guided in. We will be landing shortly. Thank you."

The purser gave us efficient words of advice. "It should not be too rough," he said, "but I suggest you take any sharp objects—fingernail files, reading glasses, pens and pencils—from your pockets. Check your seat belts, please. We suggest you hold your pillows in front of you in case it is a bit choppy. It should not be too bad. There should be no difficulty."

I wiped the moisture from the window with my hand and looked out on clouds drifting in pools of flickering light, heat lightning, we called it at home, and my father used to say it was nothing more than angels flapping their wings. A bolt of lightning—God's wrath—was different.

We started our descent, coming down full blast as if plane and crew were celebrating their victory over the storm. Nothing could happen now. Nothing would dare happen after God's wrath had been spent on us so close to His heaven. The singing sound of our approach to the runway set up a tonal line as straight and clear as a musical beam. It rang in my ears, tugged at my heart, started something in me singing, and caused the signals from the landing field to rise up like silver cushions ready to soften our fall. There was a blinding network of lights and jangled noises and then the jarring, electrifying jolt of wheels upon the earth, wheels and racing wind showering us with the shadowy sights of people and red lights whirling, and rivers of rain coming down as the brave, undaunted engines brought their precious cargo home.

We sat there looking out, reserved and silent, as if no one wanted to show his true emotion of either gratitude or fear, the natural human reaction, I suppose, of all who cross the bridge and then look back.

Soon we were taxiing to the terminal and the stewardess was saying that she appreciated our cooperation, that it was good to have had us on board, that despite the weather she hoped we would all be together again, and that there would be umbrellas and umbrella bearers for those whose flight was terminating here in Jerusalem.

The thought, rushing into my mind from nowhere, told me I had come home, back to a parental land with reels of memory spinning in my mind. A Via Dolorosa or a triumphal march, thorns or flowers, shadows or light, storm or calm, search or discovery, all were part of the game.

The Holy Land, like life, still needed to be explored and understood, and apprehension could interpret either, either way. A Prophet on a mount, a mother reciting poetry, or even a monk in Mandalay, who could say where these would lead? Who would wish to make any prediction? Around a bend a fellow goes, and right ahead he sees a rose—or perhaps a man with a clipboard in his hand.

It was all very real and very wonderful.